Critical Minded
New Approaches to Hip Hop Studies

Edited by Ellie M. Hisama and Evan Rapport

ISAM Monographs: Number 35

Institute for Studies in American Music
Brooklyn, NY

Institute for Studies in American Music
Brooklyn, NY 11210
© 2005 Institute for Studies in American Music
All rights reserved. Published 2005

ISBN (paper): 0-914678-37-X

Contents

Preface   v

"We're All Asian Really": Hip Hop's Afro-Asian Crossings
    ELLIE M. HISAMA   1

"You Ain't Heard Us 'Til You Seen Us Live": The Alter Egos'
Live Alternative to Mass Market Hip Hop
    DAVID G. PIER   23

Uptown-Downtown: Hip Hop Music in Downtown Manhattan
in the Early 1980s
    JONATHAN TOUBIN   41

Gender Dynamics in the Film *Anne B. Real*
    STEPHANIE JENSEN-MOULTON   61

Listening to the Music of the Brooklyn-based Rapper Sensational
    EVAN RAPPORT   77

Wallowing in Rupture: Cultural Hybridity, Alienation, and Andre
Benjamin's "A Life in the Day of Benjamin André (Incomplete)"
    ROBERT WOOD   95

A Preliminary Step in Exploring *Reggaetón*
    EJIMA BAKER   107

Musical Interchange between Indian Music and Hip Hop
    CARL CLEMENTS   125

Notes on Contributors   143

Preface

In Spring 2004, I taught a doctoral seminar on hip hop titled History/Theory/Criticism of Hip Hop at the Graduate Center of the City University of New York. It was the first time that such a course had ever been offered in the music program, and one of the first in the country offered at the doctoral level. The participants in the seminar were among the most talented and promising students I have ever taught. Their training in the disciplines of ethnomusicology, musicology, music theory, composition, American Studies, and anthropology generated a heady mix of perspectives on the readings, music, and films explored in the seminar. One student, Evan Rapport, proposed that we publish the seminar papers, and ultimately served as co-editor. I agreed to take on this project because of the stellar quality of the final papers, the need for scholarship in hip hop from musicians' perspectives, and the opportunity for the students in the seminar to learn how to prepare an essay for publication.

The present collection of essays, *Critical Minded: New Approaches to Hip Hop Studies,* goes beyond the usual suspects of Public Enemy and Eminem to explore New York-based Afro-Asian hip hop; the musical and social dynamics of a live hip hop band in downtown New York; hip hop's migration from the Bronx to downtown Manhattan; a film set in New York City that features an Afro-Latina rapper; an idiosyncratic Brooklyn-based African American rapper named Sensational; the African American rapper Benjamin Andre of OutKast; the rise of reggaetón (a mixture of rap and reggae); hip hop's influence on South Asian diasporic popular music and the use of Indian music in U.S.-based hip hop. We hope that the book will stimulate further scholarly work on hip hop from a multiplicity of perspectives, and will also find its way into the hands of students, scholars, and practitioners alike.

I am grateful to Evan Rapport for his dedication to the project and for his superb editing. Seminar participants Ole-Martin Ihle, Angela Lawrence, Zachary Leader, Pat Muchmore, and Ted Sammons provided valuable insights, and visits by Mark Katz and Joe Schloss were high points of the seminar. Jerry Lim contributed his talents to the book's design and layout. Thanks to Stephanie Jensen-Moulton and David Pier for proofreading the volume. We gratefully acknowledge publication support from the Diversity Projects Development Fund at the City University of New York and from Brooklyn College, City University of New York. My heartfelt thanks to the contributors for their hard work and for a great seminar.

Ellie M. Hisama
Brooklyn, New York
August 2005

"We're All Asian Really"
Hip Hop's Afro-Asian Crossings

ELLIE M. HISAMA

Enthusiasm for things Asian is evident in numerous examples of African American popular culture. In a tongue-in-cheek examination of her own Asiaphilia, Latasha Diggs writes: "Asian culture ... [comes] to us via Amazon.com as feng shui coffee table books, Shambhala pocket wisdom, and Le Chateau hot shorts made of red Chinese silk. I can read *The Art of War,* go see the Dalai Lama in Central Park, and sport my Sisqo 'Unleash the Dragon' baby tee with no ridicule" (Diggs 2003: 91). Kung fu movies have long been a fixture in black urban communities, brightly colored East Asian-themed shirts with images such as dragons or Anime characters splashed across the back are popular items in Harlem, and NBA players such as Marcus Camby display tattoos with Chinese ideograms. The Studio Museum in Harlem's 2003 exhibit *Black Belt,* of contemporary works by African American and Asian American artists, testifies to the variety of ways in which transcultural, polyethnic exchange translates into visual artistic expression (Kim et al. 2003). The spate of films in which black men and Asian men join forces—e.g., Jackie Chan and Chris Tucker in *Rush Hour* and *Rush Hour 2,* and rapper DMX and Jet Li in *Cradle 2 the Grave*—can be traced to the movie industry's desire to tap into African American communities' longstanding interest in the martial arts and kung fu culture.

Since the early 1990s, rappers including the Wu-Tang Clan, Afu-Ra, Jeru the Damaja, dead prez, and Foxy Brown have integrated elements of East Asian culture into their music, CD covers, videos, and lyrics, manufacturing an Asiaphilic trend in hip hop to which a sizeable segment of black consumers responds. Hip hop music by black rappers invokes the East by sampling dialogue from kung fu movies, using loops of traditional Asian or pseudo-Asian music, or incorporating the sound of martial arts swordplay. By exploring the visual and sonic ways in which black hip hop artists have represented East Asia and Asians, I hope to show that this particular type of cross-cultural borrowing, which Amy Abugo Ongiri has called "cultural exchange at the margins" (Ongiri 2002: 31), accomplishes an intricate kind of cultural work, one that reaches towards Asia in ways that differ from white representations.

In considering how Asians are positioned within the cultural imaginary of black hip hop, I am particularly interested in the issue of whether and how black representations of Asians diverge from white representations of Asians. In facing a different partner in a binary pairing—Asian/Black rather than Asian/White—the relationship is inflected differently. These Afro-Asian cultural crosscurrents can be linked to the 1980s trend in pop and postmodern music of representing the Orient as a passive and mystical force.[1] Yet they also diverge from these earlier models by tapping into a stream of East Asiaphilia evident in black popular culture at large. I argue that black Orientalist musical expressions in American hip hop are complex, and range from interest in learning about the Oriental Other to less benign forms of anti-Asian racism. My study concludes by exploring an example of the Afro-Asian dynamic present in the work of an Asian American rapper, Jamez, who is inspired by African American politics and culture.

JIM JARMUSCH'S 1999 FILM GHOST DOG centers on an African American man who lives according to a Japanese code of honor while working as a hit man for an Italian crime family. Despite his line of work which requires that he kill a dozen or so people a year, the protagonist is portrayed as a sympathetic character who is loyal to Louie, his employer: he loves books, encourages a young girl to read, and tends his flock of carrier pigeons by means of which he communicates with Louie. While dozing on an apartment rooftop, Ghost Dog recalls in a dream the day on which he was attacked by a trio of Italian American men. Louie saves his life, and when Ghost Dog locates him four years later, he offers his services as a hit man. The markers of Ghost Dog's identification with Asian culture are encapsulated in the rooftop scene: he has just been reading *Rashomon*; in the dream, he is shown wearing a T-shirt with kanji on it; the medallion he wears is a modified version of the symbol shown in *Hagakure,* a seventeenth-century treatise written by the samurai Yamamoto Tsunetomo, excerpts from which Ghost Dog reads aloud throughout the film; and he practices martial arts against the skyline.

Jarmusch's selection of Robert Diggs (aka RZA) to score the film is a brilliant choice. A driving force behind the wildly successful rap group Wu-Tang Clan, RZA composes an evocative instrumental score as well as the rap that is heard diegetically in different parts of the film.[2] As in the film, some aspects of the Wu's embrace of Asia are decidedly Orientalist. The cover of the Wu's 1999 CD *Wu-Chronicles* features a scowling, muscular male Asian martial artist who is balanced on one foot while standing within a ring of fire, which burns a circle around the Wu's signature sword. Along the left side of the cover, Chinese characters run alongside four I Ching symbols. The album opens with a monologue from the 1984 kung fu film *Shaolin vs. Lama.*[3]

Since their watershed album *Enter the Wu-Tang (36 Chambers)* of 1993, the Wu-Tang Clan is probably the best-known example of a group of black rappers who link themselves to Asia and Asians, and has led the way for other rappers in turning Eastward.[4] The nine members of the Wu-Tang Clan grew up in the projects of Staten Island, which they call "Shaolin," a reference to Shaolin style kung fu which is pitted against Wu-Tang sword fighting in the 1981 film *Shaolin and Wu-Tang*.[5] Members of the Wu-Tang Clan practice several styles of kung fu, and RZA, Ghostface Killah, and GZA studied chi-gong with the Shaolin monk Sifu (RZA 2005: 67). RZA links the Wu's verbal dexterity to a "martial arts" or "warrior aspect" of their music, and suggest that they are applying the "spirit of kung fu" to their lyrics (64).

Enter the Wu-Tang presents images of rough New York street life, powerful and arresting voices, signature instrumental loops, a striking palette of percussion samples, and intricate wordplay. In "Wu-Tang Clan Ain't Nuthing Ta F' Wit," an otherly Eastern-sounding world is established. It presents a brief clip from the classic 1979 film *Five Deadly Venoms* with background drone and pentatonic-derived melody. The words "tiger style," sampled from the film, launch an unrelenting sonic and verbal assault ("Like a super jet/Me fear no one, oh no, here come/The Wu-tang shogun, killer to the eardrum!").

The Wu's artistic and public personae are often difficult to untangle. In an interview with *Time* magazine, RZA notes that "...we're from the street. It's hard sometimes for the average person to come work for us. People be scared of us, man.... Say you're an accountant and you come to our office and see that many of us and you feel all this pressure not to mess up. A lot of people have resigned ... because they think 'Yo, I can't take it, I don't know if I'm gonna get punched in my face if I fuck up.' Not that we gonna punch someone in the face, but there's just a feeling of intimidation" (Eskanazi 2000b).

The Wu's interest in martial arts in the early 1990s was not completely new to the hip hop scene—breakin' or breakdancing from the 1970s includes moves from martial arts including hand spins from *capoiera*, a type of Afro-Brazilian martial arts, and the Rock Steady Crew adapted kung fu stances and gestures for some of their routines in the 1980s—but the Wu's gaze toward the Orient is much more sustained than that in earlier decades: they project "Asianness" as a central part of their identity. Their name refers to a sect of Taoism, a sword style of kung fu based in Northern China, and the sword that appears in their logo. They sample sonic clips from kung fu films and read Sun Tzu's two-thousand year old book of strategy, *The Art of War*, the I Ching, *Hagakure*, and other East Asian texts. RZA calls *The Art of War* "a beautiful book": "[L]ots of cats in the industry got into that ... I went from that to *The Art of Peace, The Sword of the Mind*, all the ninja stuff. That was when I started reading *Tao Te Ching*, the *I Ching, The Hagakure*. It all helped me out in my business and my life" (RZA 2005: 67).

Associating the group with kung fu and Chinese war strategy enhances the Wu's hard-hitting, invincible image. Their projection of a wall of manly strength is predicated upon the exclusion of women from the group, and is reinforced by misogynist lyrics in many of their tunes.[6] Because Asian men have been characteristically gendered as feminine in dominant Western representations, the

Figure 1. RZA and Sifu in China. Photo by Sophia Chang.

Wu-Tang Clan's strong identification with them is striking.

In *Common Ground: Reimagining American History,* Gary Y. Okihiro records the gendered histories of Asian men in America, arguing that

> Asians embody the geographies of the East and nonwhiteness, and the gendering that delineates "woman." ... White manliness in late-nineteenth-century America was made, in part, in the nation's imperial project in Asia and the Pacific and in the conquest by remasculinized white American men of femininized Asian and Pacific peoples, even as white womanliness and the "new" woman were enabled by Asian American men domestics, who performed feminine duties and, like women, were passive and asexual. (Okihiro 2001: xiii)

In his study of twentieth-century fiction, drama, and film, David L. Eng contends that "the Asian American male is materially and psychically feminized within the context of a larger U.S. cultural imaginary" (Eng 2001: 2). In the context of these representations as outlined by Okihiro and Eng, the Wu-Tang's invocation of the figure of the feminized Asian male may seem to contradict their steadfast allegiance to predictable presentations of black masculinity. Their unyielding hypermasculinity—of tough, streetwise black men with unmatched verbal and physical prowess—is a defining feature of how they are perceived and is key to their critical and commercial success.

In his article "Looking for My Penis: The Eroticized Asian in Gay Video Porn," Richard Fung ([1991] 1998) sketches the "totalizing stereotype of the 'Oriental'" in relation to Philippe Rushton and Anthony Bogaert's work that places Asians and blacks on opposite ends of a spectrum that purportedly measures physical factors such as size of genitalia, buttocks, and lips; Rushton and Bogaert claim that larger size of such features positively correlates to criminality and inversely with intelligence (Rushton and Bogaert 1988; cited in Fung [1991] 1998: 115-16). Fung claims that popular films consign Asian men to two basic categories: the egghead/wimp or the kung fu master/ninja/samurai: "He is sometimes dangerous, sometimes friendly, but almost always characterized by a desexualized Zen asceticism. So whereas, as Fanon tells us, 'the Negro is ... turned into a penis. He is a penis,' the Asian man is defined by a striking absence down there" (Fung [1991] 1998: 117).

Yet the Wu's longstanding respect for and interest in the work of Asian men does not contradict the image of hypermasculinity that they uniformly project. Rather, it suggests that their view of Asian men sharply contrasts with one-dimensional white constructions of them in relation to gender and sexuality. RZA emphasizes the centrality of many Asian men, including monks, philosophers, and martial artists, to the Wu-Tang's identity.[7] His insistence in aligning the Wu with such Asian male figures indicates his abiding interest in exploring alternatives to Western dominant modes of religion and philosophy, as is also evinced in the group's allegiance to the Five Percent Nation.[8]

The Wu's Afro-Asian fusions are grounded in their longstanding interest in East Asian culture and philosophy; a desire to establish a masculine, physically powerful persona for the Clan; a playful, postmodern inclination to re-present sound bites from their favorite Hong Kong action films; and a stake in creating a successful entertainment conglomerate. The Wu-Tang Clan's embrace of East Asian culture is thus both a romanticization of the Orient and a vehicle for making money. The Wu's business manager, Mitchell Diggs, who is RZA's older brother, notes that the kung fu/Shaolin mystique was instrumental to the band's success, adding that "myself, RZA and other members of the family basically focus … on constantly reinventing and finding new ways to market the logo.… We do have a lot of praise for the artist, but the artist is part of a brand. And the brand must be allowed to fly like the United States flag" (Eskenazi 2000a). When RZA traveled to China in 2000, he visited Tiananmen Square and unsuccessfully tried to put up a billboard promoting his music (Eskenazi 2000c).

The Wu's success in flying their flag is considerable: Wu Tang, Inc. grosses more than $25 million in annual sales; sales of their spin-off products (videos, videogames, and a line of shoes and clothing, Wu Wear, are flourishing, with $15 million in annual sales during the three years after their 1997 double CD *Wu-Tang Forever,* which sold 600,000 units during its first week on the market (Eskenazi 2000c; RZA 2005: 78). They have started Wu Tang Corporation and Wu-Tang Filmz, and RZA is developing a sampling machine to market to DJs. Coupled with their considerable musical talents, the Wu's deliberate self-exoticization helps to set them off from other rap groups and puts their goal of global corporate domination within reach.[9]

THE WU-TANG CLAN'S REPRESENTATIONS OF EAST ASIA are echoed in Afu-Ra's work, but with a more virulent strain that goes farther in its Orientalist appropriation of Asian male martial artist trappings. On the cover of his 2000 CD *Life Force Radio,* Afu-Ra stands in a pseudo-Asiatic pose with his eyes, shape of head, and hair Orientalized. The track "Mortal Kombat" opens with a chorus of monks chanting in what Afu-Ra calls "perverted monk style." A sinister-sounding Chinese underworld is evoked in DJ Premier's brilliant mix of a pentatonic loop, bass guitar, and drum set. Masta Killa from the Wu-Tang Clan traces a circuitous path through what might be a Wu-Tang warrior's final journey, using a virtuosic string of alliteration, assonance, and internal and end rhymes; the song later employs a racist reference to the supposedly Chinese-like eyes of a woman from the Brooklyn neighborhood of Bed-Stuy. This track demonstrates explicitly the strain of racism present in such over-the-top representations of Oriental mysticism.

Like the Wu-Tang Clan, Afu-Ra focuses on the martial arts as his primary Orientalizing gesture, but adds the more literal dimension of yellowface. When asked about his experience shooting a video in Hong Kong, he acknowledges that his view of the East is imagined: "We all have fantasies of doin' the Kung Fu every Sunday when it was on TV … And now it's like, I do Martial Arts. That's part of my life… I'm like the Rasta Jim Kelly!! Like Jet Lee and all of them, I wanna look like that. Or live up how they doin' they thing" (Black n.d.).

Figure 2. CD cover of Jeru the Damaja, *Wrath of the Math.*

Unlike his musical disciple Afu, Jeru the Damaja does not affect the pose of a stern Afro-Asian warrior on the cover of his 1996 CD *Wrath of the Math,* but stands solemnly, wearing a turquoise silk Chinese jacket trimmed in pink while rubbing what looks like a crystal ball. The photo of his 1994 CD *The Sun Rises in the East* lacks such mystical trappings, and he is in army fatigues in his 2003 CD *Divine Design.* Figure 3 gives the lyrics for "Intro (Life)," from *The Sun Rises in the East,* which opens with a lecture on the balance of opposites and references to yin and yang:

Figure 3. Excerpt from Jeru the Damaja, "Intro (Life)," *The Sun Rises in the East.*

Life is the result
of the struggle between dynamic opposites
Form and chaos
Substance and oblivion
Light and dark

And all the infinite variations of yin and yang
With occasional swings in favor of one
Eventually swings in favor of its opposite
Thus the balance of the universe is maintained

Jeru's turn toward the East suggests a more benign and less machismo connection to Asian culture than is evident in the Wu-Tang Clan's music. When asked his opinion about the conflict between East and West, Jeru replied: "I don't give a fuck about that shit because I don't come from the east or the west. We all come from the eastern hemisphere. That's just a trick that society puts up in order to divide all of us and to make us fight each other because if we knew that we all come from the same place, then there wouldn't be a reason to fight …. We all came from the East …. So we're all Asian really" (Davey D. 1996).

Foxy Brown, who takes her name from Pam Grier's character in the 1974 Blaxploitation film of the same name, demonstrates that orientalism in hip hop is not only the domain of men. On the track "The Chase" from her first CD, *Ill Na Na* of 1996, she refers to her ethnic makeup: "the Philippine black thing, you know the stee dunn/A-filiation, caramel brown/Ill style complexion, you know the deal." Figure 4 presents a portion of the lyrics from "(Holy Matrimony) Letter to the Firm" from *Ill Na Na*.[10]

Figure 4. Foxy Brown, Excerpt from "(Holy Matrimony) Letter to the Firm."

I'm like whatever for my team through the cheddah
Through the cream we gonna stay together, it's do or die
Through the slanted eyes, I organize family style
Lady Godiva, forever firm fox boogie, never lonely
We were wed in holy matrimony, whatever,
Whichever, however, uhh, firm style

Hip hop's version of "Stand By Your Man," "Letter to the Firm" declares that "I'm married to the firm boo, you got ta understand/I'll die for 'em, gimme a chair and then I'll fry for 'em/And if I gotta take the stand, I'ma lie for 'em/It's me and you, hand and hand forever."

Her second album, *Chyna Doll* (1999), blatantly offers up an exotic East Asian image. The title of *Chyna Doll* is given in pseudo-Asian script on the cover, and Chinese tattoos are visible on Foxy's right arm and left breast. Foxy's depiction of her eyes in the lyrics of several songs as "slanted" and her later persona as a black-Chinese sex diva on "Chyna Doll" is an act of both self-Orientalization—she is half-Asian and half-Trinidadian—and a deliberate conflation of Asian ethnicities—she is half-Filipina, not half-Chinese (Melesky 2002). In dressing up as an exotic half-Asian, half-black woman who is not shy about explicit sex-talk, Foxy unleashes female-specific stereotypes of Asian sexuality (Dragon Lady rather than Lotus Blossom), but updates them for twenty-first century polyethnic tastes.

Figure 5. CD cover of Foxy Brown, *Chyna Doll.*

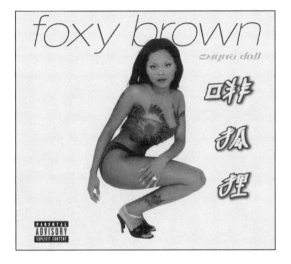

NOT ALL EXAMPLES OF AFRO-ASIAN CONNECTIONS, musical or otherwise, are Asiaphilic. Gary Okihiro (1994) presents a far-reaching history of alliances between African Americans and Asian Americans. Vijay Prashad (2001) investigates the overlapping, culturally porous histories between blacks and Asians over five centuries, tending a past borne of anti-racist struggle enacted by figures such as Malcolm X and the Japanese American activist Yuri Kochiyama. Prashad argues that while notions of cultural pluralism and diversity opened the space for the struggle against cultural homogeneity, they do not solve problems of racism because they do not attempt to dismantle privilege (63). In the realm of jazz, experimental and improvised music, and anti-racist musical activism, Fred Ho's Afro-Asian Music Ensemble brings together free jazz and traditional Chinese music; Jason Kao Hwang fuses East Asian music with jazz and experimental music in his opera *The Floating Box* (2005); and the New York-based Creative Music Convergences, which includes saxophonists Matana Roberts and Salim Washington, koto player Miya Masaoka, pianist Vijay Iyer, bassist Hakim Jami, and drummer Elliot Humberto Kavee, promotes cutting-edge music by artists across racial and ethnic lines.

The black Brooklyn-based hip hop duo dead prez weaves elements of Asian martial arts, philosophy, and war strategy into their music and image. Like Public Enemy, dead prez are activist rappers. M1 (Mutulu Olugbala, formerly Lavon

Alfred) is originally from Jamaica and grew up in Brooklyn, and Stic.man, or Stic. (Knm Olugbala, formerly Clayton Gavin) hails from Florida. In 1990 they met at Florida Agricultural and Mechanical University where M1 was a student (Phanor n.d.). After M1 joined the National People's Democratic Uhuru movement in Chicago, he and Stic. formed dead prez. The name of the group can be understood as slang for paper money as well as a call for the end of a presidential system of government.

Figure 6. dead prez (Stic. and M1). Photo by Anthony Cutajar.

Both M1 and Stic. are members of the African People's Socialist Party and disciples of Chairman Omali Yeshitela, who leads the Uhuru Movement, a grassroots Afrocentric political organization.[11] On their 2000 CD *lets get free,* two songs, "wolves" and "police state," employ samples from Yeshitela's speeches. M1 is also active in the New York branch of the National People's Democratic Uhuru Movement, organizing clothing drives, community dinners, mass rallies, and political education classes (Furqan n.d.). Many of dead prez's songs are critical of the state, the police, and politicians. Stic. remarks: "We're trying to build a movement besides music, as opposed to just a gimmick of Blackness on records ... [W]here we're coming from, we're talking about building a revolution, we're not just talking about black awareness, or positivity, or changing the school curriculum. We're talking about building black power for black people, through our daily work, and ultimately through revolution" (Semtex 1999).

lets get free is refreshingly free of the misogyny that plagues other rap music. Women are "women," not bitches and hos; dead prez have said that they think women should wear clothes that are comfortable. They are also vegetarians, and sing of the virtues of barbecue tofu, curry falafel, and lentil soup, which they call "mental fruit"; they have been known to toss apples into the audience in order to promote a healthy lifestyle (Phanor n.d.). dead prez's influences include musicians (Public Enemy, NWA, Bob Marley, Marvin Gaye), political figures (Malcolm X, the Black Panthers, Huey P. Newton), and the martial artist and actor Bruce Lee.

As a Japanese American growing up in southern Illinois, where there was no Asian community to speak of (though my mother did find dried shiitake mushrooms and azuki beans at a grocery dubiously called "Mr. Oriental"), I often found myself equated with difference. One particular marker was through the martial arts, which was omnipresent on TV and in movies. Throughout my youth, kids would come up to me on playground, hands stiffly posed in a mock karate gesture, and ask: "Do you know kung fu?" I used to ignore the question, but eventually decided that the most effective response was to nod solemnly.

Yet Asian martial arts are not always used as a weapon of racism, as it was for me, but as a weapon *against* racism. Taky Kimura, a former pupil and close friend of Bruce Lee, recalls that:

> Even while growing up in Hong Kong, Bruce ... experienced his fair share of prejudice and discrimination. This led him to become involved in the martial arts for both mental and physical self-preservation. He often spoke to me of the way the British officers looked down upon and mistreated the Chinese. From this background, Bruce swore to use the martial arts as a tool to express his ultimate desire: to create equality among the peoples of the world. (Kimura 1997: 16)

As Prashad argues, karate—the literal meaning of which is "empty hands"[12]—has taken root in many African American communities because it is accessible by working-class youth—one doesn't need expensive equipment, "just a small space, bare feet, and naked (empty) hands" (Prashad 2001: 133), as dead prez articulate in their song "Psychology" from *lets get free*: "karate means empty hands/that's why it's perfect for the poor man." Prashad further notes that kung fu "gives oppressed young people an immense sense of personal worth and the skills for collective struggle" (132).

dead prez train in jeet kune do ("The Way of the Intercepting Fist," a specialty of Bruce Lee) and in Ile-Ijala, an African system of martial arts. "We're about training in Martial Arts, so that we have some self defence," they note. "We're about stopping the police from brutalizing us every day. We're about tearing down the prison walls that hold us hostage and captive, and building programs that enable us to do that.... We're about all our rights, our rights to bear arms, our right to pursue happiness, and our right to be free" (Semtex 1999).

Another critical connection dead prez makes to Asian culture is through the I Ching (the Book of Changes), the three-thousand year old manual of divination.[13] Sony's website for dead prez identifies the I Ching as "a system ... used by the wise men and women of China some three thousand years ago as a means of analyzing reality and perfecting the art of foresight. That process of change is symbolized in [dead prez's] music and they believe there is a common link between all historically oppressed people" (dead prez n.d.).

The cover of *lets get free* and M1's tank top shown in Figure 6 reproduce their logo, which is the seventh hexagram of the I Ching.[14] This particular hexagram, "shih," is made up of the trigrams earth and water, and denotes "the conduct of military expeditions in a feudal kingdom.... the combination of lines in it is made out to suggest the idea of an army... the undivided line in the second place [from the bottom] should be interpreted of the general, who is responded to by the divided line in the fifth and royal place" (Legge 1963: 72).

The I Ching has been read by political leaders such as Mao Tse-Tung as a metaphorical guide to governing a country. As Thomas Cleary argues, "[T]he I Ching ... [and] *The Art of War* [have] an incalculable abstract reserve and metaphorical potential.... The political basis of military strength, or the social basis of the strength of any organization, is a teaching that is ... rooted in the I Ching" (Cleary 1988: 4, 8).

dead prez's commitment to I Ching in their vision of political revolution is also evident in their song "We Want Freedom," which asserts that "we represent the I Ching and to this we stand true."[15] Over a loop of a lilting flute, harp, and guitar, they trace the hard realities of life for many people and a plan for changing the system. dead prez interprets the I Ching symbol as the "people's army" that will bring about "Black revolution in the real world, not just on record. Basically we want to see our people have power over their own lives, self determination, and we think that's a right every human being on the planet should have" (Semtex 1999). For dead prez, the I Ching and martial arts are integral parts of a progressive politics.

Although African American hip hop in many cases perpetuates romantic fictions about East Asian history, philosophy, and culture, and in some cases unhelpfully reduces Asian culture to a single dimension, the strain of East Asiaphilia described here diverges from dominant musical Orientalism by whites in three ways: for the Wu-Tang Clan and Afu-Ra, it connects these rappers to the kung fu films fondly recalled from their youth and emphasizes the masculinity of the Asian male body; for Foxy Brown, the "Philippine-black caramel brown thing" allows her to establish and define the sexuality of the biracial Afro-Asian female body; and for Jeru the Damaja and dead prez, the East offers a way to reach for alternatives to Western thought.

ANOTHER TYPE OF AFRO-ASIAN HIP HOP FUSION includes Asian American rap influenced by African American culture. Asian American rap has not yet reached mainstream America, and many people are unaware that it even exists. The best known Asian American in hip hop is probably the Filipino American turntablist DJ Qbert (Robert Quitevis), who with his Invisbl Skratch Piklz crew won the DMC World DJ Competition.[16] Other Asian Americans in hip hop include the Mountain Brothers, the Kozmonautz, and Yellow Peril.[17]

Born in the Bronx in 1972, rapper Jamez is a second-generation Korean American who grew up in a suburb of Los Angeles and graduated from Bard College with degrees in sociology and multiethnic studies.[18] "Growing up as a minority," he remarks, "sometimes you feel stigmatized." He recalls that as an adolescent, he connected with other Asians, but "sometimes … I felt discriminated from whites or other groups" (English 1998). When he was fifteen, he wrote his first song, "Black Man Singing in a White Man's World."

> [I]t was a metaphor for the alienation that I, as a young Asian kid, felt but could never elegantly express—until that moment. Since Bruce Lee was dead and Margaret Cho wasn't big back then, I found my role models in the Black community. Chuck D, Run, Malcolm X, and Alex Haley guided me through adolescence and later inspired me to delve into my own roots, my own musical heritage (Chang 1999: 356).

He muses that he found black role models "since there weren't any Asian American performers out there I could readily identify with. I identified with their feelings of alienation" (English 1998).[19]

Like many other children of immigrants, Jamez at first rejected the traditional culture of his parents, but after a visit to Korea, he became interested in traditional Asian music, primarily Korean and Chinese music: "Fusing Korean folk music with Chinese music and hip hop provided the ideal social landscape I wanted to create" (English 1998). At Bard, he learned about the exploitation of Filipino and Chinese laborers in the U.S., the internment of the Japanese Americans during World War II, and other cases of anti-Asian discrimination. When Fred Ho visited Bard, he convinced Jamez to combine his interest in Asian American political issues and music.

Jamez calls his blend of traditional Asian folk music with contemporary hip hop a new genre, "Aziatic hip hop." A self-described "street musicologist" who wants to promote "cultural literacy by fusing folk music with hip hop," Jamez wants to teach young Korean Americans to reclaim their cultural traditions and identity through music, noting that "[j]ust as jazz music emerged as a uniquely African American tradition, Asian Americans are now in the midst of their own 'Asian Pacific Renaissance'" (English 1998). He hopes that his music will "inspirate the fate" of Asian Americans—that is, inspire and motivate them to develop "cultural literacy

... to be proud of their own music, then you can elevate the level of discussion of economics and politics and the military and sexism." Noting that his "best response has been from the Black community," he wants many people to "'establish the sign,' meaning have a deep appreciation for cultures that are not yours ... once that appreciation is there ... I think that there would be parity, there would be equal footing" (Baker 1996).

The title of Jamez's debut CD from 1998, *Z-Bonics*, is a play on the African American vernacular mode of speech, Ebonics. The "Z" in "Z-Bonics" is a reference to "Zipperhead," the racist term coined by American soldiers during the Korean War to refer to the supposed appearance of an Asian person's head after it is shot with a high powered rifle or run over by a Jeep. The "F.O.B." in Jamez's label, F.O.B. Productions, stands for "Fresh Off the Boat," a derogatory name for new immigrants that he wants to reclaim (Sheridan 1998).

"7-Train" is part of the score for the 1999 documentary film of the same name. The ridership of the number 7 is multiethnic and multiracial. It joins the borough of Queens to Times Square/42nd Street in midtown Manhattan, connecting Koreans and Chinese in Flushing ("New York's real K-town [Koreatown]," according to Jamez); Latinos and Latinas in Corona; Indians, Pakistanis, and Bangladeshis in Jackson Heights; Turks in Sunnyside; and Greeks and Cypriots in Astoria.

The film chronicles the events in a typical workday for a Korean manager of a fish store, a gay Pakistani sari salesman, and two Otavalen Indian street vendors. Jamez notes that "[the 7 train] represents my Flushing experience ... [my neighborhood] is unbelievably wonderful. You got Haitians, Jamaicans, Chinese, Koreans. We're just a melting fusion of voices, but there definitely is a feeling of unity, especially when I'm on the seven train ... [The song is] an ode to all those hardworking people in Queens who happen to ride on that train, especially the immigrants. The train is like a microcosm of Queens" (English 1998).

The song draws upon traditional Korean music called *p'ansori*, which is the singing of a long narrative with drum accompaniment; "pan" refers to a place where people gather together, and "sori" refers to the singing voice. Jamez calls p'ansori "rap for Koreans.... It chronicles the lives of the lower classes stigmatized, and makes fun of the upper classes through metaphor ..." (Chang 1999: 356).

Heather Willoughby links p'ansori with the concept of *han*, a "national ethos, ... ideology, emotion, and feeling" encompassing grief, pain, suffering, and regret that is supposed to underlie Korean society (Willoughby 2000: 18). Jamez writes that:

> I could identify with the sadness, the alienation, and the mourning quality of the han as expressed in P'ansori. The "tragic" quality of the han was expressed most poignantly in the weeping vibratos of the singers. Yet it was put in context, sur-

rounded by a narrative, political satire, a dialogue between the performer and her audience. P'ansori was empowering for me because it demonstrated that I could infuse my own music with deep emotive quality and yet promote a revolutionary Asian American politics simultaneously. In a sense, I transported the han from my homeland to my backyard. I had found the "resistance music" that I had been borrowing previously from Bob Dylan and Public Enemy. What my project was over the next few years was to recontexualize the music to fit my Korean American experience.[20]

Jamez's use of traditional Asian music creates what he calls a form of "anti-appropriation," or a way of reclaiming music that has been used in Western-produced kung fu films. In contrast to Afu-Ra, who draws upon Asian martial arts as an Orientalist "hook," or dead prez who want to use martial arts as a weapon in the people's army, Jamez refuses to reinscribe himself as a rappin' Karate Kid.

The reference to April 29th in the lyrics of "7-Train" shown in Figure 7 is to April 29th, 1992, the day on which four white Los Angeles police officers were acquitted of using excessive force against black motorist Rodney King.[21] The refrain suggests that "Many others forgot they own name" after the numbing commute concluding an eighteen-hour day, but are rejuvenated by the sight of a baby with her mother riding the train. The haunting, repetitive use of the refrain evokes the repeated rhythms of the train ride. The presence of the following vocal samples midway through the song, by Asian American, Latino, and African American speakers, reinforces the song's bringing together of disparate sonic and social worlds into a polycultural whole. The sampled lines that "We all Negroes/We all black" reinforce the connection not only between Koreans and black people, but among all oppressed people:

Figure 7. Jamez, excerpt from "7-Train."

[Vocal samples]
We are just looking for a place to survive
Poverty and extreme unemployment
April 29th
...
[Jamez]
Many others in a moment's time
Sacrifice Illuminate light
Many others forgot they own name
But I'm about to use it
Many others in a moment's time
Sacrifice Illuminate
Many others forgot they own name

Healing on the 7 train

[Vocal samples]
We're in search of something better
Somos una nación de inmigrantes
'Cause we all came from the same stock
We all Negroes
We all Black

   While it is important to recognize in these and other examples that black inter-est in Asian culture and Asian interest in black culture may or may not represent positive cultural trading, as Amy Ongiri notes, these exchanges "[provide] a telling moment of slippage and indeterminacy in which notions of the totalitarian nature of power and western notions of aesthetics, culture, and dominance are undone" (Ongiri 2002: 39). In other words, East Asian and African American cul-ture can offer a compelling aesthetic and cultural space in which those people who feel alienated from white mainstream U.S. society are able to explore alternative texts, metaphors, and visions. Whether we are all Asian, as Jeru declares, or whether we are all black, as Jamez suggests, or whether we decide that we consti-tute another polycultural identity altogether, perhaps this search for alternative cultural and political modes will help us to work towards a world that is not as we know it.

Acknowledgments

For their thoughtful comments on various portions of this study, I would like to thank audiences at the annual meeting of the Society for American Music, Lexington, KY, March 2002; the colloquium series of Stony Brook University's Music Department and Women's Studies Program, April 2002; the 2002-2003 Woodrow Wilson Career Enhancement Fellowship Program, retreat in Princeton, NJ, October 2002; the colloquium series of Columbia University's Music Department, December 2002; the Music Graduate Society of McGill University, Faculty of Music, March 2003; the biannual conference of the International Association for the Study of Popular Music, Montréal, July 2003; the annual meeting of the Society for Ethnomusicology, Miami, October 2003; the symposium *Listening, Hearing, and Cultural Criticism,* Program in Women's Studies and Center for the Study of Women in Society, CUNY Graduate Center, October 2004; and the graduate collo-quium series, Peabody Conservatory of Music, April 2005. I am grateful to Joseph Dubiel, Mark Katz, Maiko Kawabata, Tony Mitchell, Felicia Miyakawa, Martha Mockus, David Pier, Evan Rapport, Joseph Schloss, Dan Sonenberg, and Heather Willoughby for sharing their thoughts on this work, to Anton Vishio for encouraging me to develop this project, to Gary Okihiro and his students for their enthusiasm and suggestions, and to Jonathan Gray and Salim Washington for many helpful discussions about this research. The Woodrow Wilson National Fellowship Foundation and the Ethyle R. Wolfe Institute for the

Humanities, Brooklyn College provided the time necessary to work on this project.

Portions of this chapter were published in the Institute for Studies in American Music Newsletter XXXII/1 (Fall 2002). © 2002 Institute for Studies in American Music.
Photo of RZA and Sifu © 2005 Sophia Chang.
Cover of *Wrath of the Math* © 1996 FFRR/London Records/Warner Music.
Lyrics of "Intro (Life)" © 1994 Irving Music, Inc./Perverted Alchemist Music (BMI).
Lyrics of "(Holy Matrimony) Letter to the Firm" © 1996 Irving Music/Jumping Bean Songs (BMI).
Cover of *Chyna Doll* ©1999 Violator Records, L.L.C.
Photo of dead prez © 2000 Anthony Cutajar.
Lyrics of "7-Train" © 1998 James Chang.

Notes

1. Hisama ([1993] 2000) explores representations of East Asian women in John Cougar Mellencamp's "China Girl" of 1982, David Bowie's "China Girl" of 1983, and John Zorn's "Forbidden Fruit" of 1987. Hisama (2004) examines Zorn's representations of Asians in his Naked City CDs *Torture Garden* of 1991 and *Leng T'che* of 1992.

2. RZA scored Quentin Tarantino's *Kill Bill, Vol. 1,* and identifies this film's music as "more of a hip-hop DJ score, because it was what we call a 'pull-out' soundtrack—meaning you just pull things out of your collection that work" (RZA 2005: 213).

3. Kung fu films are a vital part of the Wu-Tang Clan's music and aesthetics (RZA 2005: 58-59).

4. *The Wu-Tang Manual* (RZA 2005) chronicles the history of the Wu-Tang Clan and reflects upon their cultural influences and philosophy. "36 chambers" in the title of their CD *Enter the Wu-Tang (36 Chambers)* is a reference to the 1978 Shaw Brothers film *The Master Killer of the Thirty-Six Chambers of Shaolin,* as is the name of Wu member Masta Killa, born Elgin Turner.

5. RZA identifies the film *Shaolin and Wu-Tang* "the best kung-fu movie I'd ever seen in my life" and admiringly remarks upon the "invincible" Wu-Tang sword style (RZA 2005: 60).

6. Imani Perry (2004) explores representations of masculinity in hip hop, including in Wu-Tang member Method Man's "All I Need" from *Tical* of 1994.

7. Such figures mentioned in *The Wu-Tang Manual* include the Buddha, Confucius, Lao Tzu, and Sifu Shi Yan-Ming, a monk who established a Shaolin temple in Manhattan (RZA 2005: 50-53).

8. All members of the Wu-Tang Clan are part of an Islamic sect known to outsiders as the Five Percent Nation or to insiders as the Nation of Gods and Earths. The Five Percent Nation of Islam was begun by Clarence 13X Smith, a former member of the Nation of Islam, and its members believe that five percent of the population understands the true knowledge of God and are not co-opted by the ten percent who control the remaining easily led eighty-five percent. RZA claims that "[a]bout 80 percent of hip-hop comes from the Five Percent" (RZA 2005: 43). Felicia Miyakawa's *Five Percenter Rap: God Hop's Music, Message, and Black Muslim Mission* (2005) explores the beliefs and work of Five Percenter rappers including the Wu-Tang Clan, Poor Righteous Teachers, Brand Nubian, and Digable

Planets.

9. RZA notes that "Wu Tang is gonna be like the Mickey Mouse ears ... Of course we gonna make money when this next record comes out ... but I'm not prepared to jump at every opportunity. It's got to be within the integrity of our brand" (Eskenazi 2000b).

10. "Ill Na Na" refers both to Foxy's nickname ("Little Mami") and to hip hop slang for the vagina.

11. For more information on the African People's Socialist Party, visit http://www.apspuhuru.org.

12. "The literal meaning of the two Japanese characters which make up the word 'karate' is 'empty hands.' This, of course, refers to the fact that karate originated as a style of self-defense which relied on the effective use of the unarmed body of its practitioner" (Nishiyama and Brown 1960: 13).

13. The I Ching is perhaps most familiar to musicians for its influence on the compositions of John Cage, who used I Ching-determined chance operations in composing the third movement of the *Concerto for Prepared Piano and Chamber Orchestra* (1950-1951), *Music of Changes* (1951), and *Imaginary Landscape No. 4* for twelve radios (1951).

14. The sixty-four hexagrams of the I Ching signify universal principles upon which people can model their lives. There are eight different trigrams, comprising three lines, either broken or solid, which indicate the yin and the yang. Each trigram represents a basic element, such as thunder, fire, or lake. Two trigrams are combined to create a hexagram, which represents various states such as progress, weakness, and good fortune.

15. dead prez's engagement with the I Ching is part of a longstanding interest by blacks in Asian political thought. Michael L. Clemons and Charles E. Jones (2001: 30) argue that the most influential revolutionary thinker impacting Black Panther doctrine was Mao Tse-Tung. Robin D.G. Kelley and Betsy Esch (1999) explore the shared political roots of black revolutionary thought and Red China.

16. Qbert's extraordinary skills can be viewed in the documentary *Scratch*.

17. For more work on Asian Americans in hip hop, see Wong 1997, Tseng 1998, Wang 1998, and Wong 2004.

18. Biographical information is based on an interview with Jamez conducted by the author in New York City on 12 November 2002, except where indicated.

19. Other important musical influences on Jamez are KRS-One, Leonard Cohen, and Bob Dylan.

20. Jamez, email to the author, 15 November 2002.

21. The verdict set off an interethnic rebellion that rocked the city. Among the thousands of buildings that were destroyed or vandalized were over 1,800 Korean-owned stores, with an estimated $300 million in property damage; many of the attacks on Asian American-owned properties were carried out by young African Americans (Marable 1995: 180).

References

Baker, Abigail. 1996. "Poongmul, Hip-Hop, and Politics: Interview with James Chang." *Yisei* (Winter). http://hcs.harvard.edu/~yisei/issues/winter_96/poongmul.html (accessed 24 February 2002).

Black, Meshack. n.d. "Afu-Ra: Decipher the Code."

http:// www.kronick.com/2.0/issue21/afu_ra.shtml (accessed 2 October 2003).

Chang, James. 1999. "Response." In *Yellow Light: The Flowering of Asian American Arts,* edited by Amy Ling, 355-61. Philadelphia: Temple University Press.

Cleary, Thomas. 1988. Translator's Introduction to Sun Tzu, *The Art of War,* 1-8. Boston: Shambhala.

Clemons, Michael L., and Charles E. Jones. 2001. "Global Solidarity: The Black Panther Party in the International Arena." In *Liberation, Imagination, and the Black Panther Party,* edited by Kathleen Cleaver and George Katsiaficas, 20-39. New York: Routledge.

Davey D. 1996. "Jeru the Damaja," www.daveyd.com/jeru.html (accessed 18 April 2002).

dead prez. n.d. http://www.sonymusic.com/labels/loud/deadprez/deadprez.html (accessed 3 July 2005).

Diggs, Latasha N. Nevada. 2003. "The Black Asianphile." In *Black Belt,* 89-95. New York: The Studio Museum in Harlem.

Eng, David L. 2001. *Racial Castration: Managing Masculinity in Asian America.* Durham: Duke University Press.

English, Merle. 1998. "Artist Finds Voice in Hip-Hop Hybrid." *Newsday,* 18 January: G03.

Eskenazi, Mike. 2000a. "Interview: Mitchell Diggs, a.k.a. Divine." *Time,* 16 November. http://www.time.com (accessed 6 March 2002).

———. 2000b. "Interview: Robert Diggs, a.k.a. the RZA." *Time,* 17 November. http://www.time.com (accessed 6 March 2002).

———. 2000c. "Remaking Wu." *Time,* 11 December, http://www.time.com (accessed 6 March 2002).

Fung, Richard. [1991] 1998. "Looking for My Penis: The Eroticized Asian in Gay Video Porn." In *Queer in Asian America,* edited by David L. Eng and Alice Y. Hom, 115-34. Philadelphia: Temple University Press.

Furqan. n.d. "Dead Prez and Their Thoughts on Revolution." http://www.nocziemi.most.org/pl/inenglish/deadprez.htm (accessed 4 February 2002).

Hisama, Ellie M. [1993] 2000. "Postcolonialism on the Make: The Music of John Mellencamp, David Bowie and John Zorn." In *Reading Pop: Approaches to Textual Analysis in Popular Music,* edited by Richard Middleton, 329-46. Oxford: Oxford University Press.

———. 2004. "John Zorn and the Postmodern Condition." In *Locating East Asia in Western Art Music,* edited by Yayoi Uno Everett and Frederick Lau, 72-84. Middletown: Wesleyan University Press.

Kelley, Robin D.G., and Betsy Esch. 1999. "Black Like Mao: Red China and Black Revolution." *Souls: A Critical Journal of Black Politics, Culture, and Society* 1: 6-41.

Kim, Christine Y., with Vijay Prashad, Latasha N. Nevada Diggs, et al. 2003. *Black Belt.* New York: The Studio Museum in Harlem.

Kimura, Taky. 1997. Foreword to Bruce Lee, *The Tao of Gung Fu: A Study in the Way of Chinese Martial Art,* edited by John Little, 15-18. Boston: Charles E. Tuttle.

Legge, James, trans. 1963. *I Ching: The Book of Changes,* 2nd ed. New York: Dover.

Marable, Manning. 1995. *Beyond Black and White: Transforming African-American Politics.* New York: Verso.

Melesky, Tom. 2002. "The Dilemma of Mixed Asians in Hip Hop." *EurasianNation.* http://www.eurasiannation.com/generic149.html (accessed 2 October 2003).

Miyakawa, Felicia M. 2005. *Five Percenter Rap: God Hop's Music, Message, and Black Muslim Mission.* Bloomington: Indiana University Press.

Nishiyama, Hidetaka, and Richard C. Brown. 1960. *Karate: The Art of "Empty Hand"*

Fighting. Boston: Charles E. Tuttle.

Okihiro, Gary Y. 1994. *Margins and Mainstreams: Asians in American History and Culture*. Seattle: University of Washington Press.

———. 2001. *Common Ground: Reimagining American History*. Princeton: Princeton University Press.

Ongiri, Amy Abugo. 2002. "'He Wanted to be Just Like Bruce Lee': African Americans, Kung Fu Theater and Cultural Exchange at the Margins." *Journal of Asian American Studies* 5(1): 31-40.

Perry, Imani. 2004. *Prophets of the Hood: Politics and Poetics in Hip Hop*. Durham: Duke University Press.

Phanor, Alexandra. n.d. "Dead Prez: Straight Revolution, No Chaser." http://www.loud.com/home/dead_prez_story_01.html (accessed 2 February 2002).

Prashad, Vijay. 2001. *Everybody was Kung Fu Fighting: Afro-Asian Connections and the Myth of Cultural Purity*. Boston: Beacon Press.

Rushton, J. Philippe, and Anthony F. Bogaert. 1988. "Race versus Social Class Difference in Sexual Behaviour: A Follow-Up Test of the r/K Dimension." *Journal of Research in Personality* 22: 259-72.

RZA, The, with Chris Norris. 2005. *The Wu-Tang Manual*. New York: Penguin.

Semtex. 1999. Interview with dead prez, 20 October 1999. http://www.djsemtex.net/interviews/deadprez.htm (accessed 1 February 2002).

Sheridan, Linda. 1998. "East Meets West for a Brand-New Groove." *Daily News*, 10 January.

Tseng, Judy. 1998. "Asian American Rap: Expression Through Alternate Forms." *Modelminority: A Guide to Asian American Empowerment*. http://www.democracyweb.com/modelminority.com/music/rap.htm (accessed 24 February 2002).

Wang, Oliver. 1998. "Asian Americans and Hip-Hop," *Asian Week*, 12-18 November. http://www.AsianWeek.com (accessed 1 February 2002).

Willoughby, Heather. 2000. "The Sound of Han: P'ansori, Timbre and a Korean Ethos of Pain and Suffering." *Yearbook for Traditional Music* 32: 17-30.

Wong, Deborah. 1997. "Just Being There: Making Asian American Musical Space in the Recording Industry." In *Musics of Multicultural America: A Study of Twelve Musical Communities*, edited by Kip Lornell and Anne K. Rasmussen, 287-316. New York: Schirmer.

———. 2004. *Speak It Louder: Asian Americans Making Music*. New York: Routledge.

Discography/Filmography

Afu-Ra. 2000. *Body of the Life Force*. Koch 8210.

———. 2002. *Life Force Radio*. Koch 8356.

Bartkowiak, Andrzej, dir. 2003. *Cradle 2 the Grave*. Warner 23294. DVD.

Bowie, David. 1983. "China Girl." On *Let's Dance*. EMI America/So 517093.

Brown, Foxy. 1996. *Ill Na Na*. Def Jam 533 684.

———. 1999. *Chyna Doll*. Def Jam 558 933.

Chang, Cheh, dir. 1979. *Five Deadly Venoms*. Entertainment Programs Interna 9981. DVD.

Cougar, John. 1982. "China Girl." On *American Fool*. Riva Records RVL 7501.

dead prez. 2000. *lets get free*. Loud 1867.

Hill, Jack, dir. 1974. *Foxy Brown*. MGM/United Artists 1001465. DVD.

Hwang, Jason Kao. 2005. *The Floating Box: A Story in Chinatown*. New World Records 80626.

Jamez. 1998. *Z-Bonics*. FOB Productions.

Jarmusch, Jim, dir. 1999. *Ghost Dog: The Way of the Samurai*. Alliance Atlantis ART 3194. VHS.

Jeru the Damaja. 1994. *The Sun Rises in the East*. PayDay/FFRR 124 011.

———. 1996. *Wrath of the Math*. PayDay/FFRR 124 119.

———. 2003. *Divine Design*. Ashenafi.

Lee, Tso Nam, dir. 1984. *Shaolin vs. Lama*. Ground Zero. DVD.

Liu, Chia Hui, dir. 1981. *Shaolin and Wu Tang*. Xenon. DVD.

Method Man. 1994. *Tical*. Def Jam 23839.

Naked City. 1991. *Torture Garden*. Toy's Factory TFCK-88557.

———. 1992. *Leng Tch'e*. Toy's Factory TFCK-88604.

Park, Hye-Jung, and J. T. Takagi, dir. *The #7 Train: An Immigrant Journey*. Third World Newsreel. VHS.

Pray, Doug, dir. 2002. *Scratch*. Palm Pictures 30462. DVD.

Ratner, Brett, dir. 1998. *Rush Hour*. New Line. DVD.

———. 2001. *Rush Hour 2*. New Line Home Entertainment. DVD.

Tarantino, Quentin, dir. 2003. *Kill Bill, Vol. 1*. Miramax. DVD.

Wu-Tang Clan. 1993. *Enter the Wu-Tang (36 Chambers)*. RCA 66358.

———. 1997. *Wu-Tang Forever*. RCA 66905.

———. 1999. *Wu-Chronicles*. Wu-Tang Records P2 51143.

Zorn, John. 1987. "Forbidden Fruit." On *Spillane*. Nonesuch 79172.

"You Ain't Heard Us 'Til You Seen Us Live"
The Alter Egos' Live Alternative to Mass Market Hip Hop

DAVID G. PIER

Most rap grooves on the radio are made up of pre-recorded sound clips which have been modified, layered, and looped with a computer. There are similarities between this process of composing grooves and the older process in hip hop of using turntables to spin *breakbeats*. A *break* is a length of danceable groove a DJ discovers on a vinyl record.[1] To make a breakbeat, a DJ loops this length of groove by alternating between two copies of the same record which spin on two turntables. When the needle is near the end of the break on one record, the DJ switches to the other record, which is cued to the beginning of the same break. The mechanically looped sound clip is one of the authentic sounds of hip hop. Mechanically looped grooves often sound as though they could only have been made with a computer or a turntable. Most producers do not attempt to replicate the grooves of live bands (Schloss 2004: 42).

Human/machine collaborations and confrontations have been important in all hip hop genres. Graffiti writers threw their signatures up on subway trains, risking their own flesh-and-blood bodies to mark up the giant metal ones. Their round bubble letters and scribbled tags stood out against the clean machine forms of the trains. The graffiti writers also experimented with scripts inspired by the primitive computer fonts of the day, set ablaze with color. Breakdancers imitated the jerky moves of robots; beatboxers did vocal imitations of cranked-up radios and drum machines; DJs made a spectacle of doing forbidden things to turntables and records—manhandling them, scratching them.[2] Hip hop innovator Afrika Bambaataa drew inspiration from Kraftwerk, a German group with an amusingly sterile electronic funk aesthetic (Toop 1998). Rappers name-checked their technologies: the microphone, the turntables, and the TR-808 drum machine. Perhaps above all, hip hop artists have relished mechanically looped "human" sounds. DJs looped the same five seconds of Lyn Collins's song "Think About It," in which James Brown shouts (as I hear it) "Yeah!" and then "Whoo!" (Douglas 2001).[3] Brown's two shouts—utterances as primally human as they come—were caused by mechanical means to echo indefinitely, without fading. This has been a highly productive opposition in hip hop: warm-blooded fallible humans colliding and meshing with cold-blooded perfect machines.[4]

Groove-keeping live bands—which never produce loops as mechanical-sounding as those made with a computer or a pair of turntables—have always seemed out of place in hip hop. Today's purist hip hop producers use live instruments, if at all, only in a "supporting capacity" (Schloss 2004: 69). On *Follow the Leader,* the seminal MC, Rakim, rapped "we don't have a band: it's just my voice and his hands, that's how hip hop was, it still stands." A few famous early hip hop groups, such as the Sugarhill Gang, used bands—in some cases only because reactionary studio producers insisted on them (Keyes 2002: 68). Since the earliest days of hip hop only one live-band act—The Roots—has achieved substantial commercial success on the mass market. Rap is not the only pop music genre to move away from groove-keeping bands; all the other offspring genres of disco have been similarly wedded to the machine aesthetic. In no other pop genre, however, has the contrast between human funk and silicon funk been so pronounced and so fruitful.

Mechanically looped beats are unshakeable. A computer, tape, or turntable motor will never get tired, drunk, or angry. It will not falter, rush or drag, or do anything pleasantly or unpleasantly surprising during a performance. This is more true of programmed beats than it is of turntable beats, since a DJ *can* make mistakes and throw in creative touches. Even with DJ accompaniment, however, there is always the fixed and unresponsive element of the pre-recorded break. A break originally performed by Clyde Stubblefield, the "funky drummer," will be just as funky now as it was on the day it was recorded. For a listener like me—who became musically aware just before mechanically looped beats became ubiquitous—these pristine repetitions still have a strange (not necessarily unpleasant) quality. They are simultaneously compelling and inert.

In the frame of performance, a mechanically looped beat need not have the same kind of presence that a band has. It can be an environmental element, like the lighting in a photograph. The mechanically looped beat can be an important part of the listening experience—it can even be the whole point—but its effect need not be attached to a human presence. By contrast, whenever a band is involved in groove-making, it is likely that social relations of some kind will dominate the frame—relations between band members, between leaders and accompanists, and between the performers and the audience. A groove is likely to be perceived as a conversation, rather than as a setting. To draw an example from another genre: *swing,* in jazz, is commonly understood as a social product. Musicians and fans think of swinging or non-swinging moments as spontaneous distillations of the musicians' personal relationships. If the musicians do not know each other well, or have been arguing, or aren't getting paid, the audience expects the groove to be affected one way or the other. This is an important mystique in jazz—whether the swing actually reflects social realities in any predictable way is beside the point. Likewise, when we go to hear funk, country, or rock bands, or classical music orchestras—or when we listen to their records—many of us pay attention to, or imagine, social relationships.

The mechanically looped beat in rap facilitates (though it does not necessitate) the isolation of the rapper's personality in the frame. Donning headphones or cranking up the surround sound in an acoustically insulated car, the listener—like an eavesdropper—enters into the rapper's private space. No band—not even an anonymous studio band—intrudes on this intimate communion. The sense of a private space generated by a mechanically looped beat is different from that generated during a solo performance *a cappella* or with self-accompaniment. The mechanical beat serves as an environment, separate from both the rapper and the listener, in which they wander together—the listener an unseen presence at the rapper's side.

Today's mass market rap is dominated by fantasies of money, sex, and revenge. In the private space a consumer imagines he or she shares with the rap star (a mechanical loop-based sound environment), he or she perhaps feels more at liberty to dwell on such subjects. Eminem, for example, is a master at narrating as though he were writing in his secret diary. His lyrics, such as those on *The Marshall Mathers LP*, are full of tortured self-analyses, revenge fantasies, and homophobic jitters.[5] Even in the midst of his most paranoid, repulsive diatribes, one senses the vulnerability of a diary confession. All the sneering machismo only serves to intensify the sense that one has snuck into a young man's private space in which he is essentially defenseless. Rap in this style—as the music industry knows full well—is a perfect music for adolescent boys isolated in suburban developments all over America. In the course of the genre's rapid rise into the mainstream and thus into the suburbs, rap has evolved from being a music mostly about partying and the neighborhood, to being a music about subjects such as the rapper's bitterness towards his mother. It has been inward-bound, shifting from the social to the psychological. Rap like Eminem's, in this way, resembles the introverted and even "paranoiac" (Kubik 1999: 33) blues of Skip James, Robert Johnson, and others. What is new is the relentless mechanical presence.

Of course, not all rap emphasizes the solitary voice. Rap performance can be—and often is—collaborative: rappers sometimes rap in groups, "trading phrases" (Keyes 2002: 62), battling, and so on. Likewise, consumers can and do dance and otherwise socialize to the sounds of Eminem. However, these kinds of social interaction in both the production stages and the consumption stages of the music seem to be less normative than they were in earlier hip hop. It is common for the star rapper to be left alone with a mechanically looped beat, and it is common for consumers to listen to rap through headphones. Certainly, the music is admirably suited to this kind of consumption. The music industry, which makes most of its money selling fantasies wrapped around star personalities, has profited from hip hop's introspective trajectory, and has no doubt shaped it considerably.

Paul Gilroy asserts that commercial hip hop, with its typical human/machine aesthetic, and its emphasis on the individual star, is characterized by an erasure of visible, spontaneous negotiations between performers. In his view, "performance" is distinguishable from "pseudo-performance" by its "assertion of real time" and "face-to-face interaction" (Gilroy 1995: 24). When performers face off in real time in front of an audience that understands what is at stake, "immediacy and proximity reemerge as ethically charged features of social interaction" (24). The bandstand or the dance circle is a site where various kinds of social relationships may be metaphorically played out. The outcomes are not assured but are decided, as in a courtroom, before an audience.

According to Gilroy, this public working-out of relationships is blocked in today's spectacle-driven concerts. Unscripted interaction is discouraged among the performers on stage, as well as between the performers and the audience. The rap live show is nothing more than "the decaying half-life of its own video incarnation" (25). In Gilroy's view, mainstream hip hop is especially prone to "pseudo-performance" because of its mechanically looped beats. He considers crucial "the difference between sampling a break that someone else created and playing a break on your own in the living collusive circle of an audience that comprehends its dynamics" (25). A mechanically looped groove might sound much like a human-looped one, but it is "pseudo-performance," because the computer risked nothing in performing it—it is not a product of relationships being worked out spontaneously that could easily go awry. Such reliability is convenient for corporate producers of concerts and records, who can promote performers based on their looks and charisma rather than their musical skills, and still put out a danceable musical product.

One can find some validity in Gilroy's assessment of current mass market hip hop and still appreciate hip hop made with computers. I will not argue that hip hop ought to be more like bebop, funk, or any other genre in which collective groove-keeping by bands is the norm. Rap that fixates on private fantasy worlds can be stimulating art, precisely because it takes us places other genres cannot. It is simply worth noting that this is the main trajectory mass market rap has taken in recent years. If the music industry has embraced the internal monologue potential of rap, and trimmed it of its sociable aspects, one might expect to find sociability—or real "performance" in Gilroy's sense of the term—being emphatically reincorporated into hip hop on the street level. This, in fact, is what seems to be happening. One local response to the anti-social trajectory of superculture hip hop has been to introduce into the genre forms of live performance which, some purists would argue, do not belong there.

ON THE LOCAL NEW YORK CITY MUSIC SCENE, one can find a surprising number of live hip hop bands. Live hip hop bands, which are poorly represented in the mass market, often present themselves as going against the grain of mass market hip hop. On one of their record covers, the New York band Alter Egos style themselves

"Defenders of Live Hip Hop." Brian Salter (aka B Salt), the rapper for the Alter Egos, explained his concept of "alter egos" to me, partly in terms of what the band does *not* do:

> I act, I write, I sing, and I dance. Rashida sings all of these different styles from classical to jazz to R&B. The guys play all of these different styles of music. And it goes back to how we were discussing ordinary conventions of hip hop and the ordinary avenues that people take. Basically, I don't want to subvert all of these other selves of ourselves simply to fit into these avenues. I want to do the opposite and infuse all of these separate selves into the greater Alter Ego collective. So that when you see the Alter Ego stage show you don't just see posturing, grabbin' crotch, playin' music, and "Peace, we're out! Thank you." But you're gonna laugh, you're gonna cry, you're gonna have a good time.[6]

Thus, according to Brian, the Alter Egos want to draw a wide range of responses from an audience, by putting the interactions between diverse, unconcealed personalities on display.

Brian teaches rap writing classes to elementary school kids in Harlem. One of his teaching goals is to get them to open up in front of class and share something of themselves through their rhymes. He has come to believe that many problems in the African American community stem from depictions in rap of black males as macho and inexpressive. Brian wants the Alter Egos to explore, as his students do, alternatives to the machismo and other kinds of egotism he hears in mass market hip hop:

> All of us weren't always the coolest people in school. All of us weren't always so cool with the girls. We need to be able to convey that without alienating and to get that truth across. I don't care what it is: as long as it's true and sincere it will be well received.

Brian was excited about the recent addition of a woman to the band—Rashida Bryant, a conservatory-trained singer with a powerful R&B voice.

> The fact that there's now this estrogen thing going on in there too: it gives us a lot more content: relationships, you know? Now we can explore ... OK, we're doing this thing on, you know, *sexual dysfunction* and all of this stuff. We couldn't have really done that ... *as easily* ... with me and Eli [another rapper, formerly with the Alter Egos]. 'Cause that's male/female stuff. It would have had to have been male/male perception of female stuff. We can do stories between a mother and son. We can even do things where *I'll* be the female and *she'll* be the guy ... just to fuck with people!

Rashida told me that she does not mind being the group's new representative of femaleness or the "estrogen thing."[7] She thinks that she, more than other women, is able to "carry it off," thanks to her commanding stage presence and voice. She would not have joined the band if she thought she would end up being "just a chick who sings." She claims to have changed the implications of songs such as "Butter Face." When Brian and his former rapping partner used to perform "Butter Face" together, it was, according to Rashida, a "kind of chauvinistic" extended joke about women with sexually desirable bodies but undesirable faces ("butter face" is a pun on "but her face"). Now, when the Alter Egos perform "Butter Face," Rashida prefaces the rap with a statement such as "OK ladies and gentlemen, little B Salt is going to tell a story about his love life problems," and concludes the song with a "moral to the story" which is likewise intended to explain the song in terms of male sexual insecurity.[8]

Rashida's membership has had an impact on the band's rehearsal politics. Tony told me that the band has been bickering less in rehearsals since Rashida joined— the men are "on their best behavior."[9] Rashida concurred: "I took the mommy role. Get your act together! Is there a goal that we're working for or what?" Besides playing the disciplinarian mother, Rashida has taken on the task of improving some of the men's personal appearances. She doesn't mind playing stereotypically feminine roles because she is confident of her ability to take charge when she wants to: "The guys are pretty much in the background [when I want them to be]. My presence is so strong that they just don't really have a chance. They can't *not* pay attention to me."

During one Alter Egos rehearsal in a warehouse in Long Island City, Brian was getting an impromptu lesson in vocal production from Rashida. Brian told me he has trouble making it through a whole set of rapping without losing his breath. Rashida is trying to teach Brian the more efficient ways she herself acquired through her classical training of supporting and directing the voice. As Brian and Rashida were talking about diaphragm support on one side of the room, the three accompanying instrumentalists—Tony Melone (aka Mel One) on keyboards, Josh Arenberg (aka A Rock) on drums, and Mike Herscher on bass—were trying to figure out a groove for the next tune. It reminded me of any number of band rehearsals I have attended: a steady stream of amiable bickering and noodling on instruments.

The Alter Egos have a consistent method of composing songs together. Tony, Mike, and Josh work out a groove collectively in rehearsal. Once they settle on something they like, Tony, the keyboardist, records it. Then Brian takes the recording home, and writes lyrics to it. In rehearsal, while the band is figuring out the groove, Brian might improvise a few rhymes to see if the groove is suitable for rapping. Or he might try to work out with Rashida a call-and-response interaction that suits the groove. Much of the time at the rehearsals I attended, the instrumentalists concentrated on composing the groove while Brian and Rashida either sat quietly or worked out their own parts.

When Tony and Brian started working together, their production process did not involve a live band. Tony and a DJ produced beats on his computer for Brian to rap over. They eventually brought in Josh and Mike—a drummer and a bassist—because a live rhythm section allowed them to get work done faster: Tony told me that it would take him days to work out a decent beat on his computer, whereas a live drummer and bass player could improvise something on the fly. Brian says that collective improvisation of this kind is important in the composing process, but that on stage he and the band prefer to sound tight and rehearsed.

I witnessed the composition of the aforementioned "sexual dysfunction song."[10] The hook to this song is "when you're hot you're hot, and when you're not you're not." The chorus has a rapid-fire exchange between Rashida and Brian:

> Rashida (enthusiastically): Oooh!
> Brian: Aah!
> R: Ooh!
> B: AAAAH!
> R (less enthusiastically): Oh.

This exchange is followed by an improvised squabble in which Brian defends his manhood and Rashida refuses to help him feel better. Brian and Rashida's comedic improvising during the rehearsal got the rest of the Alter Egos charged up. Josh, the drummer, suggested that the band sonically simulate Brian's detumescence by means of a *ritardando* and descending bass *glissando*. The band tried this musical trick a few times, then scrapped it.

All of the instrumentalists in the Alter Egos are conservatory-trained jazz musicians. Especially in the early days of his work with the Alter Egos, Brian was intimidated by the fact that the instrumentalists spoke a standard music conservatory language and he didn't. Over time, he has picked up and put to use some of their concepts and terminology. He explained to me:

> At first? Oh, trying to work with them, I had no idea what they were talking about half the time. It was just two different worlds, it really, really was. And now I can completely understand when they say "come in on *one*." I *get it* for the most part. Whereas before I had to stop. Or if they said "come in on the *and of one*"... I still don't exactly know what that means but I can feel what they're talking about. I don't know if the *and of one* is *before* or *after* the one but I know it's somewhere there. That knowledge has different uses when I'm writing, but most of it is afterthought cause the feeling is always there. 'Cause what we're talking about is just how do you talk about it after it's said and done?

Brian says that the easiest beat to rap over is a sparse, simple one. If he has a recurrent gripe, it is that the instrumentalists play too much and leave him too little room. He thinks that perhaps they play complicated figures because, as jazz musicians, they would be bored by anything simpler. He has complained to the instrumentalists about their busy playing, but they have not always heeded him. Loud and busy playing seems to be a recurrent problem; in one rehearsal, Rashida made insistent hand motions to the band to play softer. Tony also thinks the band needs to leave more space for the vocals. He admitted that all of the instrumentalists in the Alter Egos, including himself, have at various times acted condescending or dismissive toward Brian in rehearsals because of Brian's lack of formal musical training. Brian's initial unfamiliarity with the kinds of concepts and terms the instrumentalists used, in addition to the fact that he did not attend a conservatory or play an instrument, put him at a political disadvantage. He has, however, appreciated opportunities to learn new musical concepts from the jazz musicians.

Brian commented on the song "Five" (on *Defenders of Live Hip Hop)*, which is in a five-beat meter:

> Something that the guys introduced to me is a five-bar [five-beat] phrase which is hard to rap over and as far as I know no one's ever really tried to flow over that. I really took that as a challenge: "Whoa, that's something that we can innovate and do something cool with." So I took it and it took me a long time to understand it. Then to understand it, to feel it. I'd go to sleep and I would play it—like as I was sleeping so it would kind of get into my subliminal. I guess my toe would be tapping as I would be sleeping or something. I did that for a few weeks and eventually one day I was like, Eureka! I can actually not have to count 1 ... 2 ... 3 ... 4 ... 5. I could actually just feel it and then I just started writing to it. And that's probably the song that I'm most proud of because it's not a sparse beat at all; it's very busy, and you know, it's five! At the same time I managed to flow over it pretty seamlessly—and not just saying one or two words per bar but just flowin' from one to the next to the next to the next.

When I talked to Tony about "Five," he seemed somewhat less enthusiastic about the song than Brian. He doesn't see a future for the Alter Egos in what he considers a kind of jazz-nerdish experimentation. Tony told me that when the band first played the odd meter groove, they were just messing around—there was no plan to turn it into a song. It was Brian who insisted on trying to rap over the odd groove.

I have chosen to concentrate on "Five" as an example of what can result from a rap production process that involves spontaneous, collaborative composition and groove-keeping. The instrumentalists were messing around with a musical pattern in a quirky meter, which caught Brian's attention. He insisted on trying to rap over it, perhaps partly to demonstrate his musical competence to the jazz musicians. Eventually Brian trained himself to rap in the lopsided meter, and thus gained a new rhythmic sensibility. His experimental approach to the five-beat meter is worth analyzing in detail. Little has been written so far about the specific rhythmic techniques of rapping. "Five" gives us a chance to consider how one rapper adapts his existing techniques to an unfamiliar rhythmic challenge.

Figure 1 shows the lyrics of Brian's rap on "Five."

Figure 1. Lyrics of "Five."

> Y'all wanna go where the Egos
> Y'all can't go where the Egos
> Egos go where nobody go
>
> One two three four five
> Egos we got to keep it live
> Notice that we're not just two MCs
> But also backed by bass drums and keys
> Through soothin' music infuse it and use it to
> Talk to us so you can choose to do a new thing
> Make ya say "Hey!"
>
> One two three four five six seven eight nine ten
> Y'all can't believe what the Egos just done did
> Bring it back with a new syntax
> That melts in your brain and makes you relax
> Wait not yet
> I gots to live gots to give
> Before I'm rottin' in a coffin
> My ancestors picked cotton
> Forgotten but not in my mind
> Journey through time
>
> Inertia will invert ya jerk ya
> Quick to the turf a the circumstances
> Of questions and answers
> Increases the chances of survivin' certain cancers
> One two three four five
> You ain't heard us till you seen us live
> Five four three two one
> That's when you see the vibratin' drum
> Say one two three four one

You takin a trip with the Mel
One two three four five
A Rock is always keepin' the time
One two three four five
Mel Rock Lee Salt Mike
One two three one two
Once just see whatcha gwan do
Mike Herscher will bring the pain
It will enable you to break the rain

Brian makes his lyrics rhythmically interesting in a variety of ways. In his rapping style on "Five," there are not many varieties of durations between syllable onsets: the times between syllable onsets could all be represented more or less accurately with eighth, quarter, and sixteenth notes or rests. Of course, Brian's rap, like most human musical utterances, is characterized by impossible-to-transcribe microvariations of duration, which make the rap swing and constitute part of Brian's individual rhythmic style (Keil 1966). Much of the rhythmic appeal of Brian's rap, however, comes not from variations in durations of and between syllables, but from variations in the ways these durations are grouped. In this respect the rhythm of his rap is similar to that of a bebop solo by Bud Powell or any other bebop musician who plays long strings of eighth notes grouped in interesting ways.

Figure 2 shows the way Brian fits these lyrics rhythmically over the beat.[11] The columns numbered 1-10 represent equal divisions of a consistent measure of time marked by a repeating pattern in the bass and drums. Each row represents one measure. Syllables in bold are syllables I hear as stressed.

Three rhythmic features of Brian's rap on "Five" are described below.

1. Various groupings by stress. With a few exceptions, all of the syllables Brian stresses in his rap would normally receive stress in speech. Two exceptions are "**an-ces**-tors" (Figure 2: measure B14), and "vib-**rat**-in" (measure C8). In each of these cases, the middle syllable receives abnormal stress.[12] If Brian wants to establish a rhythmic pattern of stresses—say, consecutive groups of three syllables, with the first syllable of each receiving stress—he tends to choose words that have the appropriate stress structures, or else he changes the rhythmic placement of syllables so that syllables that are stressed in normal speech receive stress according to the established rhythmic pattern. For example, in measure B10 he compacts "can't believe" so that the normally accented syllable "-**lieve**" falls on an odd numbered (typically stressed) column. Brian's lexical choices and his rhythmic choices are thus, unsurprisingly, interdependent.

Figure 2. Analysis of the rhythm in Brian Salter's rap over the Alter Ego's "Five." Syllables in bold are stressed. Measures in the grouping column marked with grey shading involve double-time (see pages 35-36).

measure	Grouping by stress:	1	2	3	4	5	6	7	8	9	10
A1		Y'all		wan-	na	go		where	the	E-	
A2		gos		Y'all		can't		go		where	the
A3		E-		gos		E-	dy	gos		go	
A4		Where	no-		bo-		dy				
B1	22222	**One**		two		three	**keep**	four	live	five	
B2	3223	**E-**	gos	we've	we	**not**	just	It	M-	C's	
B3	22222	**No-**	tice	that	we				and	keys	
B4	3232	**But**		so	backed	**by**	**bass**	drums	and	keys	
B5	2233	**Through**		soo-	thin	**mus-**	ic	in-	fuse	it	and
B6	3322	**use**		to	talk	**a**	to	us	so	you	can
B7	3223	**choose**		to	do	**a**	**new**	new	thing	it	
B8	235	**Make**	ya	say		**a**	**hey**		**thing**		
B9	4444	**One**	**two**	**three**	**four**	**five**	**six**	**se-** ven	**eight**	**nine**	**ten**
B10	4444	**Ya'll**	can't	be lieve		e-	gos	just	done	did	
B11	4444	**Bring**	it	back	with	the	new	syn- tax	that	melts	your
B12	35444	**brain**	and	makes	a	re- new		Wait	not	yet	in
B13	33344	**I**	gots	in	to		fin	give	be-	fore	I'm
B14	2231(2+	**rot-**	tin	ton	a	cof-	fin	my	an-	ces-	tors
B15	1)333	**picked**	cot-	ton	for-	got-	ten	but		in	my
B16	235	**mind**		Jour-	ney	through	time				
					CHORUS (repeat A1-A4)						
C1	22222	**Quick**	I-	ner-	tia	will	in-	vert	ya	jerk	ya
C2	332(2+	of	to	the	turf	a	the	cir-	cum-	stanc-	es
C3	1)333	**chan-**	ces	tions	and	an-	swers	ad-	vanc-	es	the
C4	22222	**One**		two	sur-	three	in	four	tain	can-	cers
C5	22222	**You**	ain't	heard	us	three	you	seen	us	live	
C6	22222	**Five**		four		three		two		one	
C7	22222		when you	two		three		drum		one	
C8	4444	**That's**		see	the vib-	rat-	in	drum		say	
C9	22222	**One**		two	what	three	in	four		say	
C10	2332	**You**		tak-		a	trip	with		Mel	
C11	22222	**One**		two		three		four		five	
C12	3232	**A-**	rock	is	al-	ways	keep-	in	the	five	
C13	22222	**One**		two		three		four		time	
C14	22222	**Mel**		Rock		three	Lee	Salt	us	five	
C15	22222	**once**		two		three		one		Mike	
C16	22222	**once**	just	see		what	cha	gwan		two	
C17	2322((1+	**Mike**		Her-	scher	will	cha	the	pain	do	
C18	2)2222	**will**	en-	a-	ble	you	to	break	the	rain	it

The ten time units that make up a standard measure in "Five" can be divided evenly into groups of two and three in seven different ways:

```
2 2 2 2 2
2 2 3 3
2 3 2 3
3 2 2 3
2 3 3 2
3 2 3 2
3 3 2 2
```

In measures B1-B7, Brian uses stressed syllables to group the ten divisions of the measure in five different ways, (out of the possible seven listed above): 22222, 3223, 3232, 2233, and 3322. Each measure's grouping is shown in Figure 2 in the column to the left of the lyrics. I assume that a stressed syllable begins a new rhythmic group, usually of two or three time units. Brian leaves the second halves of measures B8 and B16 empty of syllables. In keeping with my rule of starting new groups at stressed syllables, I have called a stressed syllable followed by four empty columns a group of five. In fact, one is less inclined to hear a grouping of five durations here, and more inclined to project the grouping of the first five columns (23) onto the second five columns.

Any grouping of twos and threes other than the seven listed above will not fit into the ten spaces: the last group will cross over into the next measure. I have indicated where this occurs with parentheses. The indicator "(2+", in measure C2, does not mean a group of two—it means a group of three that begins in measure C2 and ends in measure C3. For example, in measure C2, the third (stressed) syllable of "circumstances" is the beginning of a three-syllable group, the last (unstressed) syllable of which comes at the beginning of measure C3. Going "over the bar line" in this way challenges the ear's capacity to keep track of the five-beat cycle.[13]

Measure B14 presents the ear with a puzzle. After the three-syllable group "cof-fin my," we expect the next syllable to be stressed, since we do not expect groups of more than three syllables. "An-" of "ancestors" is stressed, but it is followed immediately by a stronger stress on "-cest-." The syllable "-cest-" becomes the first syllable in a chain of three-syllable groups. Thus "an-," which we expected to be the beginning of a new rhythmic group, turns out to be a false start. In the grouping column I have marked "an-" as a one-syllable group. The strength of "an-" as a probable beginning, both because it is the stressed syllable of "ancestors" in normal speech, and because it comes after a three-syllable group, causes a temporary disorientation, as the ear tries to figure out whether the abnormally stressed "-cest-" should indeed override "an-" as a new group beginning.

2. Various groupings by rhyme. In the melodic chorus (Figure 2, rows A1-A4), and throughout Brian's rap, we see the technique, ubiquitous in rap, of rhyming not just at the ends of lines, but insistently and with rhythmic inventiveness within lines: e.g., "E-*gos go* where *no*-bo-dy *goes*," and, in Figure 2, measures B14 and B15, "I *gots* to live, *gots* to give before I'm *rot*-tin' in a *cof*-fin my an-ces-tors picked *cot*-ton for-*got*-ten but *not* in my mind." Note that in the latter example "an-ces-tors"—which, as I have argued above already presents the ear with a puzzling break in the rhythmic stress pattern—also breaks the established pattern of *-ot/-off* rhymes on stressed syllables. The importance of rapid chains of rhyming syllables in rap is obvious. Less obvious, and worthy of further consideration, are the ways rhyming syllables, separated by greater expanses of time and contrasting material, subtly reinforce one another. Arguably, the *cotton-coffin-forgotten* rhyme chain is anticipated and prepared for earlier in the rap with the lines such as "egos we *got* to keep it live" (measure B2) and "notice that we *not* just two MC's" (measure B3).

3. Six against five cross-rhythm. The melodic chorus, shown in Figure 2, rows A1-A4, consists of three repetitions of a six-beat rhythmic phrase superimposed on a five-beat meter. Figure 3 shows the six-beat parallel phrases vertically aligned. The five-beat meter on which these phrases are superimposed is counted above the staff.

Figure 3. Six against five cross-rhythm.

Y'all wan-na go where the E - gos Y'all can't go where the   E-gos E-gos go   where no-bo-dy go

4. Double-time. *Double-time* and *half-time* are terms Brian brought up. These are common terms in jazz: double-time is the effect of doubling the number of divisions one feels in a given measure of time. In rap, double-time would mean fitting twice as many syllables (or rests where syllables could be) in the same amount of time. In measure B1, Brian raps "One two three four five." In B9, he marks the beginning of the double-time feel by rapping "one two three four five six seven eight nine ten." The word "seven" (two syllables in the space of one column) prepares a new subdivision of the beat: rather than ten time units, there are now twenty time units available within the same measure of time. Figure 2 shows that Brian stays in double-time in measures B10-B13, then resumes the original meter in measure B14. These double-time measures are shaded grey in the grouping column. "44444" is the double-time equivalent of "22222" because the same columns end up stressed. Note that in measures B12 and B13, Brian uses stresses to subdivide the measure as it can only be subdivided in double-time, splitting the twenty divisions into 35444 and then 333344.

"Five," like other Alter Egos songs, emerged out of a loosely controlled environment of improvisation and exchange among musicians. Keeping the odd-metered groove was a challenge for the band members to take on collectively: the possibility always loomed that someone might mistakenly count an extra beat and mess everyone else up. Brian especially took on this challenge with enthusiasm, perhaps partly because he felt a need to prove his musical skills to the conservatory-trained jazz musicians. Authority is clearly an important asset in the collective negotiations of rehearsals and performances. The band members, with their analytical language and experience in jazz and funk performance, possess one kind of authority. Brian, on the other hand, as the rapper, has the authority that comes with being more of a hip hop insider and the person at the front of the stage. As I noted earlier, both the men and Rashida herself ascribe some of her authority to her presence as a woman and as a new member of the band. She also possesses her conservatory training, her presence at the front of the stage, and the powers of her voice and personality as sources of authority. Racial perceptions must figure into this equation as well: Brian and Rashida, as the two blacks in an otherwise white ensemble, probably wield some authority linked to their blackness, since hip hop is a genre strongly associated with blackness.

The lyrics of "Five" are about the band (in its pre-Rashida incarnation) as a collective of five musicians. The individual musicians are lauded for their contributions: "A Rock is always keepin' the time" (C12), "You takin' a trip with the Mel" (C10), but then amalgamated in a single measure: "Mel Rock Lee Salt Mike" (C14). The lyrics stress reciprocal communications through music: "through soothin' music, infuse it, and use it to talk to us so you can choose to do a new thing" (B5). The potency of the live performance experience ("that's when you see the vibratin' drum" [C8]) is opposed to "inertia" (C1), which is associated with a history of racial oppression ("before I'm rottin' in a coffin, my ancestors picked cotton, forgotten but not in my mind" [B13-16]).

The audible involvement of a live band complements the political rhetoric in the lyrics. The relationships Brian dwells on in his lyrics are mirrored in the performance relationships. An audience member encountering the Alter Egos for the first time will not have been present at the long rehearsals and hang-out sessions that led up to the gig—he or she will have missed the arguments as well as the moments of reconciliation—yet he or she will likely sense that political negotiations have occurred and are occurring even in the present moment. Something of the band's history can be read in the individuals' facial expressions and body movements: a grin here, an admonishing look there. Attuned listeners can hear conversations in the sonic fabric: a slightly-too-assertive bass line here, an enthusiastic group acceleration there. There is in an Alter Egos performance a richness of musical variables describable in terms of human interactions (e.g. "she's not leaving him enough space," "he's listening to her," "he's pushing them") which one does not commonly find in mechanical loop-based hip hop. These musical conversations give even the Alter Egos' recordings an essence of liveness.

WHILE THE ALTER EGOS DEFINE THEMSELVES to some extent in opposition to super-culture hip hop with its macho themes and antisocial fantasy sphere, they are not out to change hip hop so much as provide an alternative to it. They are all lovers of mainstream hip hop, and, despite their use of the hip hop label, they are reluctant to categorize their product as pure hip hop. Like so many bands, they prefer to describe themselves as occupying some as yet undefined space between several genres—jazz, R&B, hip hop, etc. In general, genre boundaries are more tightly policed in the mass market than they are in their local manifestations. I suspect the prevalence of live hip hop bands in New York has to do with the many jazz musicians in the city. All of the live hip hop bands I have found are, like the Alter Egos, made up mostly of musicians versed in bebop. Many jazz musicians are drawn to hip hop, and hip hop musicians are drawn to jazz. At the weekly jazz jam session at Niagara in the East Village, it is not uncommon for a visiting rapper to step up to the microphone and freestyle over a few choruses of a bebop standard such as "Alone Together."[14]

The plentitude of live hip hop bands in New York may be partly understood as a critical response to the mass market. As I have suggested, mass market hip hop has become a music centered on the inflated personal histories and psychologies of stars. Local live hip hop bands like the Alter Egos put complicated social negotiations back in the frame. They thus offer hip hop fans something they are not getting much of from other pop culture sources: models for collective action. Those of us lucky enough to have grown up participating in bands, orchestras, or choruses know the value of the political as well as musical education one gets in rehearsals and concerts. Even if one does not participate directly in performance ensembles, one can learn politics by watching and listening to bands. Different ensembles offer different models for political action: the suave aristocracy of the Duke Ellington orchestra is one political model, the lockstep funk of James Brown's band is another, the amiable disorganization of the Grateful Dead is yet another. Disturbingly, the media giants seem to be increasingly uninterested in showing ensemble interactivities. Stars appear in videos with their posses, but the performance interactions among them are minimized. More often than not, the star appears alone in the frame, so that the viewer at home can fantasize an intimate connection between him or herself and the star. What kind of politics does this kind of entertainment foster?

It is heartening to remember that the mass market version of a genre is never the whole story. Local groups like the Alter Egos are inspired by mass market rap, but they also purposefully diverge from it. If spontaneous collective performance has been weeded out of mainstream hip hop and replaced with individualistic fantasy and Gilroy's "pseudo-performance," it may be that "real" collective performance is being asserted more forcefully than ever in subcultural versions of hip hop.

Acknowledgments

Thanks to the Alter Egos for their music and their thoughtful self-reflections, and thanks to Ellie Hisama, Evan Rapport, and Stephen Blum for being keen and patient readers and continual sources of inspiration.

Lyrics and transcriptions are printed with the permission of Alter Egos.

Notes

1. According to Joseph G. Schloss, the term *break* is also used more broadly to refer to "*any* segment of music (usually four measures or less) that could be sampled and repeated" (Schloss 2004: 36). Thus, a *break* need not necessarily include a good beat or be on vinyl.

2. For more on DJing techniques, see the 2002 documentary *Scratch*. For more on graffiti writing and breakdancing, see the documentary *Style Wars*.

3. This break can be heard, for example, on Rob Base and DJ EZ Rock's "It Takes Two."

4. Brown's shouts, mechanically looped, acquire a strange and inhuman fixity, like that of the original Echo's voice:

Her voice and bones are all that's left; and then
her voice alone: her bones, they say, were turned
to stone. (Ovid 1993: 93)

The disturbing and yet compelling effect of mechanically looping a human (and more specifically, African American) shout was explored by Steve Reich in his apocalyptic 1965 tape piece "It's Gonna Rain." The "break" in Reich's piece is a few seconds of the sermon of a preacher named Brother Walter.

5. A talented role player, Eminem has not relied solely on the tortured, introverted persona, though it is arguably this character who put him on the map. In his recent anti-Bush propaganda piece "Mosh" (from *Encore*) his rapping is much more extroverted and political, in the style of Chuck D or KRS-One.

6. This and all other comments from Brian Salter in this paper come from an interview conducted by the author on 21 April 2004.

7. Comments from Rashida Bryant come from an interview with the author conducted on 3 July 2004.

8. Whether or not Rashida succeeds in making "Butter Face" seem any less chauvinistic by explaining to the audience that the song is about male sexual insecurity, she does succeed in making "Butter Face" seem like a more appropriate song for the Alter Egos to perform. When the song was performed by Brian and Eli, their dirty joke was conspiratorial: an audience member was required to either join them in the intimate circle of the macho joke, or detach herself from the performance. This forced decision was at odds with the inclusive, live atmosphere the Alter Egos otherwise generated. Rashida's preface reconstructs Brian's conspiratorial joke as a morality play, upon which the audience is invited to collectively pass judgment.

9. Comments from Tony Melone come from an interview with the author conducted on 26 April 2004.

10. To my knowledge, this song has not yet been recorded.

11. Brian approved of this way of transcribing his rap and helped me correct errors in my transcription of his lyrics.

12. That is, stress that is abnormal in so-called standard English. Brian, like most rappers, makes pointed use of various "black" idioms. See Figure 2, measure C16: "once just see whatcha gwan do." The stresses in "ancestors" and "vibratin'," may be similarly significant.

13. Odd-metered grooves such as five and seven, relatively rare as they are in Western popular music, are notoriously challenging to keep track of. Any straying from the fixed measure may cause a performer to lose track of the orienting "one" beat.

14. More information about the jam session at Niagara is available at www.gregglassman.com. I have been the house pianist at the session since 2002.

References

Douglas, Adam. 2001. "These are the Breaks." http://formen.ign.com/news/29351.html.

Gilroy, Paul. 1995. "'… To Be Real': The Dissident Forms of Black Expressive Culture." In *Let's Get It On: The Politics of Black Performance*, edited by Catherine Ugwu, 12-33. Seattle: Bay Press.

Keil, Charles M. 1966. "Motion and Feeling through Music." *Journal of Aesthetics and Art Criticism* 24:33-49.

Keyes, Cheryl L. 2002. *Rap Music and Street Consciousness.* Urbana, IL: University of Illinois Press.

Kubik, Gerhard. 1999. *Africa and the Blues.* Jackson, MS: University of Mississippi Press.

Ovid. 1993. *The Metamorphoses of Ovid.* Translated and edited by Allen Mandelbaum. New York: Harcourt Brace & Company.

Reich, Steve. 2000. "Steve Reich: Early Tape Pieces; Interview by Jason Gross." http://www.furious.com/perfect/ohm/reich2.html.

Schloss, Joseph G. 2004. *Making Beats: The Art of Sample-Based Hip-Hop.* Middletown, CT: Wesleyan University Press.

Toop, David. 1998. "The A to Z of Electro." http://www.jahsonic.com/DavidToopElectro.html.

Discography/Filmography

Alter Egos. 2003. *Defenders of Live Hip Hop.* http://www.checktheegos.com.
Eminem. 2000. *The Marshall Mathers LP.* Interscope 490629.
———. 2004. *Encore.* Aftermath 377172.
Eric B and Rakim. 1988. *Follow the Leader.* Uni Records UNID-3.
Pray, Doug, dir. 2002. *Scratch.* Palm Pictures 30462. DVD.
Reich, Steve. 1992. *Early Works.* Nonesuch 79169.
Rob Base and DJ EZ Rock. 1990. *It Takes Two.* Profile 1267.
Silver, Tony, dir. [1983] 2003. *Style Wars.* Plexifilm 40007. DVD.

Uptown-Downtown
Hip Hop Music in Downtown Manhattan in the Early 1980s

JONATHAN TOUBIN

No matter black white or brown in our own way we can all get down.
—Grandmaster Flash and The Furious Five, "Freedom"

During the most segregated period of pop radio since the 1940s, the early 1980s,[1] a number of rap, punk, and new wave songs deliberately crossed racial and cultural boundaries. Blondie's "Rapture" and the Clash's "The Magnificent Seven," both from 1980, are two of the first recorded examples of punk and new wave acts incorporating hip hop elements into their songs. Conversely, Grandmaster Flash and the Furious Five's "It's Nasty" and Dr. Jeckyll and Mr. Hyde's "Genius Rap," both from 1981, are based on samples from new wave band Tom Tom Club's 1981 track "Genius of Love." The Clash's "Overwhelmed by Funk" from 1982 features a rap by uptown graffiti writer/rapper Futura 2000. DJ Afrika Bambaataa and punk vocalist Johnny Lydon performed a duet on their 1983 apocalyptic dance-floor hit "World Destruction." 1982's "Planet Rock" is the product of Bambaataa and MCs Soul Sonic Force with white dance music producers Arthur Baker and Tommy Silverman and keyboardist John Robie. The most popular breaking hit of the era, jazz legend Herbie Hancock's "Rockit" from 1983, was born out of Hancock's interracial, intercultural collaboration with DJ Grandmixer D.St. and producer/bassist Bill Laswell.

Each of these examples sprouted directly out of alliances formed in lower Manhattan's art and club scenes. After years of relatively isolated development in the Bronx and Harlem in the 1970s, hip hop rapidly became a downtown fixture in the early 1980s. Along with breaking and graffiti, the music not only served as a bridge between two polar geographic regions of New York, but also between people of different races, ethnicities, classes, subcultures, and musical tastes.[2] MCs and DJs appeared on stages and on bills with new wave, experimental, and punk bands. Breaking crews were the star attractions at large nightclubs, art galleries, and public festivals. The work of graffiti writers shared museum and gallery walls with canvases by popular neo-expressionist artists. Uptown residents were going downtown and, to a lesser extent, downtown residents were going uptown, to witness the new spectacles. Afrika Bambaataa recalls his first experience with the new diverse audience:

> When I got down there, and I started playing all that funky music, you seen them
> punk people start going crazy! Slam-banging, jumping crazy, with the hip-hop

people looking at them like, "What's this?" Then you see the hip-hoppers trying
to do that punk dance and that thing where they're going side to side, and then
the punks trying to do the rap steps and all this sort of stuff. (Fricke and Ahearn
2002: 309)

While graffiti, breaking, DJing, and MCing left a stamp on lower Manhattan's
art and club scenes, the four elements of hip hop[3] were also affected by downtown
culture. In addition to the artistic benefits of new outside influences, the
uptown/downtown nexus was also mutually profitable economically. In what DJ
Jazzy Jay refers to as "the Great Hip Hop Drought," when hip hop's Bronx audience
was shrinking as members got too old for parties at high school gyms, parks, and
community centers, going downtown provided graffiti artists, breakdancers, rappers, and MCs with a new expanded market for their art.[4] Downtown galleries,
clubs, and artists financially and culturally profited from their association with the
new trends. The press had something new to write about. The underground art,
dance, music and film scenes of lower Manhattan were also hip hop culture's
points of contact with the mainstream art, dance, music, and film industries.

Hip hop's journey downtown can be told as a story of the removal of geographical and cultural barriers between groups of people. Here I explore these formative
years between hip hop's initial isolation in the Bronx and its later explosion
around the world. I will argue that hip hop's voyage downtown and into the mainstream was brought about by the persistent efforts of a few people. These protagonists were a small, loosely knit group of artists, performers, gallery owners,
promoters, and journalists. This study will be limited to the period that begins
with the Funky 4+1's first show in at the Kitchen in Soho in 1980 (Fricke and
Ahearn 2002: 216) and ends with the formation of Def Jam Records in 1984.
While uptown and downtown artists certainly interacted before 1980, particularly
in the realm of graffiti, the Kitchen show is the first documented live hip hop performance downtown. The founding of Def Jam provides a perfect bookend for the
era because it marks the point where the concepts of uptown and downtown are
no longer necessary in understanding the relationship between rappers and
their audiences.

Escape From the Bronx

In the beginning, hip hop music existed primarily in the Bronx. Kool Herc's
performance at his sister's birthday party in 1973 marks the point at which most
publications date the beginning of hip hop music (Fricke and Ahearn 2002: 23-43;
Keyes 2002: 55-57; Light 1999: 14-15). Herc's primary contribution was his discovery of the "breakbeat," in which the DJ extends the drum break by alternating

back and forth between two copies of the same record. His second important contribution was his MC crew, the Herculords. Herc's work with breakbeats and MCs was further articulated by followers such as Afrika Bambaataa and Grandmaster Flash. The Bronx's DJs, MCs, breakdancers, and graffiti writers helped create what had become a substantial subculture in the South and West Bronx by the late 1970s. By this point Harlem disco DJs such as Eddie Cheeba and DJ Hollywood began incorporating Bronx hip hop music styles into their acts ("Rap Records" 1980). A young Russell Simmons, after his introduction to hip hop via a performance by Cheeba and Easy G at Charles' Gallery in Harlem in 1977, started RUSH productions and began booking hip hop acts into high school gyms, fraternity houses, neighborhood community centers, and nightclubs in Harlem and Queens, and, soon, lower Manhattan (Simmons 2001: 34). By 1979, Kurtis Blow, already under the management of Simmons, brought hip hop performance outside of the New York metropolitan area and into major east coast cities (George et al. 1985: xii).

While social and geographic isolation kept live hip hop music from being heard outside of black and Puerto Rican communities, an absence of commercial recordings kept the music off of the air and out of the stores. Over the six-year period from 1973, when Kool Herc began DJing at block parties, to 1979, the year Fatback Band's "King Tim III (Personality Jock)" was released, not one commercial rap recording appeared on vinyl.[5] Homemade audiocassettes were hip hop's primary release medium during the genre's formative years. Home recordings and live tapes were sold on the streets and at performances. These cassettes and their pirated duplicates not only reached other parts of the city, but also other parts of the country. The tapes were heard in New York's parks, streets, and subways through large portable radios, or "ghetto blasters," that were fashionable among urban youth (Keyes 2002: 67).

Sylvia Robinson of Sugar Hill Records got the idea of releasing rap on vinyl after noticing how popular the homemade tapes were with her nieces in New Jersey. These cassettes indirectly led to Sugar Hill's first release, a song that reached #4 on the R&B charts and broke into the Top 40, Sugarhill Gang's "Rapper's Delight" from 1979.[6] Also in 1979, the first major label rap release—Kurtis Blow's "Christmas Rapping" on Mercury—sold 600,000 copies and made the R&B charts. Local independent labels such as Enjoy and Winley began releasing the first recordings of artists such as Grandmaster Flash and the Furious Five, Afrika Bambaataa and Soul Sonic Force, the Funky 4+1, the Treacherous Three, and Spoonie Gee.[7] Because all of the artists except for Kurtis Blow had releases on independent labels, rap's early recordings were often difficult for potential customers to find (Keller 2004). The first hip hop radio show did not appear until "Mr. Magic's Rap Attack" appeared on Newark's WHBI in 1979 (Keyes 2002: 72-73).

Despite the Bronx's isolation, homemade tapes, ghetto blasters, a handful of vinyl releases, a smattering of radio play, occasional rotation at discos, and word of mouth randomly transmitted the area's music across the geographic, social, and economic boundaries of New York. Afrika Bambaataa recalls meeting East Village residents who were familiar with his music through mixtapes when he debuted downtown in 1981.[8] Mike D of the Beastie Boys heard hip hop music for the first time from a mix tape at his high school (Keller 2004). Producer Arthur Baker witnessed live DJs and MCs at a park in Harlem in the late 1970s ("Archive Interviews: Arthur Baker" 2004). In an email interview conducted 1 October 2004, Bad Seeds percussionist Jim Sclavunos informed me that he witnessed a Rock Steady Crew subway performance long before he appeared in the Kitchen Tour with them in 1982. While downtown did not see a live performance until 1980, a number of downtowners found hip hop before it found them.

The Art Scene

Visual art, music, and dance were so deeply intertwined in hip hop music's introduction to the downtown club scene that the genre's southern migration cannot be understood outside of the context of graffiti and breaking. The Mudd Club, Club 57, Danceteria, and other clubs that began popping up in the late 1970s were unlike many of their predecessors in that "people didn't just dance and do drugs and hob nob." Jean-Michel Basquiat's biographer Phoebe Hoban explains that "they were venues for performance art, underground films, New Wave music … Artists were mixing up their media; music, film, painting, and fashion were recombining in innovative ways" (Hoban 1998: 9). This is the context in which hip hop music downtown must be viewed. Before it came into its own downtown, the music functioned as a soundtrack for the more popular elements of graffiti and breaking. Not only did the early success of graffiti and breaking downtown help create a market for the music, but at the Kitchen, the Mudd Club, Negril, and later at Danceteria and the Roxy, MCing and DJing were often presented as part of a spectacle that involved all four elements.

While a number of downtowners were aware of uptown graffiti, breaking, and hip hop music, an exponentially broader recognition of the movement was created by the physical placement of graffiti artists, b-boys, DJs, and MCs in downtown venues. Members of downtown's art scene, such as Fred "Fab 5 Freddy" Braithwaite, Henry Chalfant, Patti Astor, Charlie Ahearn, and Michael Holman, played a more important role than figures from the music community in hip hop's downtown migration. Graffiti had appeared sporadically in art galleries since the United Graffiti Artists (UGA) exhibit at the Razor Gallery in 1973 (Austin 2001: 72). By traveling daily across hundreds of miles of subway tracks, graffiti, of the four elements, was witnessed by the greatest diversity of people. With a heterogeneous assortment of practitioners, graffiti's ability to cross racial, geographical, and gender lines enabled it to connect geographically and culturally separated people.

The downtown galleries' direct predecessor in commingling the emerging uptown and downtown art scenes was the Bronx art gallery Fashion Moda. Downtowner Stefan Eins opened the space in a South Bronx storefront in 1978 as "a means of communication beyond ideology" that connected "the street ... with the international art world" (Webster 1996). Along with a number of Bronx graffiti writers and downtown artists, punk rockers Charlie Ahearn and his brother John both exhibited at Fashion Moda in 1979. Charlie Ahearn, who later went on to direct the 1982 hip hop movie *Wild Style,* exhibited his 1979 film *The Deadly Art of Survival* and John Ahearn created an installation of plaster casts of Bronx residents in "South Bronx Hall of Fame." A performance by graffiti writer Phase II's Bronx rap crew the Wicked Wizards in 1979 was perhaps the first hip hop music performance in an art gallery. Also, in a reversal of the later trend at the Kitchen and the Mudd Club, downtowners the Relentless Blues Band commuted uptown to perform (Webster 1996). In October 1980, nineteen year-old graffiti writer Crash curated the exhibit "Graffiti Art Success for America" featuring his friends Lady Pink, Futura, Ali, Zephyr and Fab 5 Freddy ("Guide to the Fashion Moda Archive" 2003). Collaborative Projects, or Colab, a downtown socio-political art collective founded in 1977, co-curated, in conjunction with Fashion Moda, the "Times Square Show" in June of 1980. Located in an abandoned massage parlor in Times Square, the exhibit included a mix of uptown and downtown artists (Frank and McKinzie 1987: 28; Hager 1986: 111). Fashion Moda's intermingling of the uptown and downtown was a catalyst for later downtown Manhattan activity.

Fab 5 Freddy and Friends and More Friends

If there is a common thread in the narratives of the of the fusion of hip hop and downtown art, it is Fab 5 Freddy. A point of origin or a point of intersection for almost every important early downtown hip hop alliance can be located within his New York crisscrossings. Grandmaster Flash explains Fab 5's role in bringing hip hop downtown:

> Fab was like one of the town criers. He would come into the hood where whites wouldn't come and then go downtown to where whites would go, and say, "Listen, there's some music these cats is playing, man. It's hot shit, you gotta book these guys. So I got my first taste of playing for an audience that wasn't typically black, you know, which broadened my horizons musically." (Chang 2004)

A graffiti writer from Brooklyn, Fab 5 Freddy became notorious for his 1980 subway homage to Warhol—Campbell's soup cans painted across the 5 Train (Hoban 1998: 36). Braithwaite wanted to make inroads into both the Bronx graffiti and lower Manhattan art scenes and consequently sought out acquaintances such as Blondie, Charlie Ahearn, and *Interview* editor/Mudd Club curator Glenn O'Brien downtown, and Lady Pink, Grandmaster Flash, and the Rock Steady Crew uptown. He was quick to recognize the parallels between the hip hop and punk scenes:

> Both were reactions against disco, both had affectations for S&M leather gear, both had musical styles derived from late-sixties records, both were youth movements despised by middle class. In fact, CBGB had a parallel club in the South Bronx called The Black Door. Even more remarkable—the two scenes knew next to nothing about each other. (Hager 1986: 107)

Braithwaite's vision for fusing hip hop elements ran parallel to that of the multimedia aesthetic of the emerging downtown clubs.[9] The downtown scene not only often mixed various media, but also different styles. This combination of stylistic eclecticism and formal variety is perhaps best illustrated by the lists of names that appeared along side one another at downtown events. The advertised bill for the 1981 "Kitchen Birthday Party" includes not only Fab 5 Freddy and Friends, but also performances by contemporary composers Steve Reich and Glenn Branca, rock bands Devo and DNA, dance troupes Douglass Dunn Dancers and the Bebe Miller Dancers, comedians Dan Ackroyd and Eric Bogosian, writer Terry Southern, and roughly a dozen more acts ("Kitchen Birthday Party" advertisement 1981). The Mudd Club combined its upstairs art gallery and downstairs performance space for similar results. Advertised as "the best in hip-hop rap music produced by Fab 5 Freddy featuring the top turntable technologists and rap vocalists on the South Bronx scene," Braithwaite's "Rapper Night" took place in the performance room of the Mudd Club in 1981 (Mudd Club advertisement 1981). "Beyond Words," billed as an "Art Show of All Major Graffiti Artists," co-curated by Keith Haring, Braithwaite, and Futura 2000, opened in the Mudd Club's upstairs gallery on the same night. In addition to exhibiting the top names in graffiti, "Beyond Words" included works by artists from other styles and media including Iggy Pop, Alan Vega, Martha Cooper, and Charlie Ahearn. True to the diverse spirit of the Mudd Club, "Rapper Night" and "Beyond Words" were scheduled between Glenn O' Brien's "Heavy Metal Night" and a performance by Sun Records rockabilly legend Sleepy LaBeef. The downtown aesthetic of eclecticism that reigned in the early 1980s found in hip hop yet another genre to throw into the mix. While a number of patrons had trouble getting past the ropes outside the

Mudd Club, these new uptown art, music, and dance forms had no problem gaining admittance.[10]

Blondie: Spreading the Rap(ture)

In addition to bringing uptown acts downtown, Fab 5 Freddy also brought a number of downtowners uptown. After Glenn O'Brien introduced him to Blondie members Deborah Harry and Chris Stein, Braithwaite arranged to take the trio uptown for a hip hop event at the Police Athletic League in the Bronx. Stein and Harry were taken by the new sound and incorporated some of its elements into a track on their new record, *Autoamerican* (1980) (Fricke and Ahearn 2002: 283). "Rapture" topped both the American and British charts (Light 1999: 48). At a time when only a handful of hip hop singles had hit the market, Harry's rhymes became many listeners' first exposure to rap. In addition to helping popularize the genre, the song's references to Grandmaster Flash and Fab 5 Freddy aroused the general public's curiosity—establishing the two as the most prominent names in hip hop.

In 1980, Blondie was at the peak of its popularity and one of the most famous bands in the world. Its celebrity and influence made the group hip hop's most powerful ally in these formative years. The band's role in the growth of the genre did not end with "Rapture." After witnessing the Funky 4+1 at the Kitchen, Harry invited the young quintet to make a guest appearance in an upcoming broadcast of "Saturday Night Live." The 14 February 1981 broadcast was the first rap performance in television history ("Saturday Night" n.d.; Light 1999: 178; Fricke and Ahearn 2002: 216). Additionally, Fab 5 Freddy became a frequent guest performer at Blondie's arena concerts and Kurtis Blow was awarded the support slot in Blondie's 1980 British tour (Light 1999: 46). Blondie was thus not only responsible for bringing rap into mainstream consciousness at the top of the pop radio charts, but also for introducing live hip hop music on national television, the arena stage, and overseas.

Legitimacy: Galleries, Performance Spaces, and Documentaries

Sculpter/photograher Henry Chalfant, an acquaintance of Braithwaite, began obsessively photographing graffiti as early as 1976 (Fricke and Ahearn 2002: 299). Originally displayed at OK Harris gallery under the exhibit title "Graffiti in New York" in 1980, Chalfant's graffiti photography also appears in the pages of the seminal 1984 book *Subway Art* (Chalfant and Cooper 1984). Finding his Soho studio transformed into "a salon for graffiti artists" Chalfant soon branched out into the world of dance when he asked graffiti writer Take 1 "if he'd ever heard of breaking" (Fricke and Ahearn 2002: 299). The next day Take 1 returned with

Crazy Legs and Frosty Freeze of the Rock Steady Crew in tow. Chalfant organized a breaking event at the Common Ground performance space in Soho featuring Rock Steady Crew, Fab 5 Freddy, and Rammellzee. The promotion for the Common Ground show resulted in a *Village Voice* cover story titled "Breaking is Hard to Do" by Chalfant's friend dance critic Sally Banes (Banes 1981). Though the Common Ground show was cancelled at the last minute, it not only inspired the first breaking cover story in a major publication, but its preparation created stronger links between the breaking, graffiti, and downtown art communities (Fricke and Ahearn 2002: 299-306).

Later in 1981 Chalfant organized a breaking contest between the Rock Steady Crew and the Dynamic Rockers at Lincoln Center's Out of Doors festival. The prestige of the event not only helped legitimize breaking, but also introduced it to new segments of New York's population (Fricke and Ahearn 2002: 299-306). Chalfant's greatest contribution to the transmission of hip hop was his work with Tony Silver in creating the first hip hop documentary, *Style Wars*. Initially filming as an independent production in 1981, the program was picked up by Public Broadcasting System and aired nationally in January 1984 (Fricke and Ahearn 2002: 300; Light 1999: 40, 56). The soundtrack is peppered with songs by crews such Grandmaster Flash and the Furious Five, the Treacherous Three, and the Fearless Four. In addition to providing the general public with a glimpse into hip hop culture, Chalfant's efforts to legitimize graffiti and breaking also helped promote the accompanying music.

Independent film star Patti Astor also played an important role in introducing hip hop culture downtown through the art world. Along with Bill Stelling, Astor opened the Fun Gallery on East 10th Street in 1981. The site of important early solo shows for Kenny Scharf and Jean-Michel Basquiat, Fun featured one-man shows by graffiti writers. The idea for Fun grew out of Astor's exhibition of a mural in her apartment by Futura 2000. Tracing the origin of Fun, Astor states, "The beginning of the Fun was when I met Fab 5 Freddy" ("Patti Astor Interview" 2002). Becoming what journalist Steve Hager labeled "the most influential gallery in New York" (Hager 1986: 110), Fun not only curated one-man shows for Fab 5 Freddy, Dondi, Lee Quiñones, Zephyr and dozens of other graffiti writers, but also became a favorite downtown hangout for DJs, MCs, and breakers.

Wild Style: Uniting the Elements, Uniting New York

Another important connection to Fab 5 Freddy was Charlie Ahearn. Through Fashion Moda and Colab, Ahearn, like Braithwaite, had been participating in both the uptown and downtown art scenes. Fab 5 Freddy met Ahearn at the screening of his kung fu movie *The Deadly Art of Survival*:

He said, "I've been looking for you, but I thought you were black" and he wanted to get together with me and make a movie. So he learned that I was really interested in Lee. He said, "I work with Lee, I'm good friends with Lee. I'll bring him tomorrow." And I said, "If you come here with Lee tomorrow, I'll give you $50 and you can put a big graffiti mural out." Which they did. And when they came, we were like okay let's make a movie together. That was June of 1980. ("Archive Interviews: Charlie Ahearn" 2001)

The movie that Braithwaite suggested became *Wild Style*. While the graffiti and murals of Lee Quiñones were well known and respected in the streets of New York, he was at this point unknown in the art scene ("Archive Interviews: Charlie Ahearn" 2001). Within a few weeks of the encounter, Fab 5 Freddy had introduced Ahearn to the Bronx hip hop scene (Fricke and Ahearn 2002: 290). Consequently, Grandmaster Flash, Cold Crush Brothers, Busy Bee, Fantastic Freaks, Double Trouble (KK Rockwell and Lil' Rodney Cee from Funky 4+1), Rammellzee, Lady Pink, and Rock Steady Crew all make appearances in *Wild Style*.

Resulting from a collaboration between uptowners and downtowners, *Wild Style* also contains an uptown/downtown theme. The plot leads the protagonist, Zoro, a Bronx graffiti writer played by Quiñones, through the Bronx hip hop world and downtown art scene. In one sequence, Virginia, played by Patti Astor, drives uptown to see the work of Zoro on a tip from Fab 5 Freddy. She brings Busy Bee, Freddy, and Zoro back downtown to a gallery opening with her and introduces them to the patrons. Virginia commissions Zoro to paint the East River Amphitheater in Manhattan's Lower East Side. Despite name changes, the actors reenact their own personal roles in the uptown/downtown story. Ties to Blondie are highlighted by the band's music pumping out of Virginia's car speakers on her way uptown and Chris Stein's soundtrack work with Fab 5 Freddy. The movie culminates with an event at the amphitheater in which rappers and breakdancers perform in front of Zoro's new downtown mural.

The process of Ahearn and Braithwaite's creation of *Wild Style* between 1980 and 1982 strengthened the ties between hip hop's elements and solidified the scene. More importantly, as his introduction of Blondie to hip hop resulted in pop radio, television, and arena audience's first exposure to rap, Braithwaite's bringing together of Ahearn, Quiñones, and the Bronx hip hop scene culminated in hip hop's first appearance in front of an international cinema audience.

Wheels of Steel: Hip Hop Rules the Night

Two figures associated with the Rock Steady Crew—Michael Holman and Kool Lady Blue—played an important role in the creation of a downtown hip hop market. After Michael Holman brought Malcolm McLaren to the Bronx River Projects to witness a Zulu Nation jam in 1981, the punk impresario asked Holman to coordinate a hip hop performance to open for Bow Wow Wow at the Ritz (Brewster and Broughton 2000: 248). After witnessing Holman's spectacle featuring the Zulu Nation DJs and MCs with the Rock Steady Crew, Kool Lady Blue, a former associate of McLaren and Vivien Westwood, asked Holman to help her coordinate a hip hop event (Brewster and Broughton 2000: 250). While Patti Astor began arranging hip hop performances in the East Village at the Fun Gallery, Holman and Blue began promoting a Thursday hip hop night around the corner at the small basement reggae club on Second Avenue named Negril that came to be known as "Wheels of Steel." While the weekly featured attraction was the Rock Steady Crew, Afrika Bambaataa, Grandmixer D.St., and other Bronx DJs began developing a downtown following at Negril (Fricke and Ahearn 2002: 302, 309). Combining live graffiti writing, breaking, MCing, and DJing, the event developed into New York's most important regular hip hop event.

Outgrowing Negril in 1982, the party relocated to the more spacious Danceteria on West 21st Street. After only a few short months of existence, the event found its final home at the Roxy, a cavernous former roller rink on West 18th Street. By this point three- to four-thousand patrons, a heterogeneous mix of uptown and downtown audiences, were attending Blue and Holman's spectacle.[11] Inflated by celebrity visitors and a barrage of media coverage, the "Wheels of Steel" nights propelled hip hop into the mainstream. Out of the large and diverse crowd, unlikely alliances were forged—for example, between uptowner Grandmaster D.St. and downtowner Bill Laswell, two of the forces behind Herbie Hancock's "Rockit" (Prasad 1999; Quan 2004). The high level of direct exposure to powerful forces in the art, entertainment, and media industries resulted in new opportunities such as Rock Steady Crew's appearance in the blockbuster film *Flashdance* (Fricke and Ahearn 2002: 302).

Hip Hop a la Carte: Music Venues and the Press

In addition to art galleries and nightclubs, hip hop was also appearing in live music venues. The first such concert was Sugar Hill Records' "Ritz Rap Party" at the Ritz on East 11th Street in 1981. The show featured a cross-section of the New Jersey label's stable of talent: Sugarhill Gang, Grandmaster Flash and the Furious Five, Spoonie Gee, Funky 4+1, and The Sequence ("Ritz Rap Party" advertisement 1981). The presentation of hip hop music at a live music venue instead of a dance club or gallery drew another audience altogether. The "predominantly white, enthusiastic crowd" (Palmer 1981a) included journalists Robert Palmer, Robert Christgau, and Vince Aletti, all of whom wrote about the show (Christgau 1981;

Aletti 1981). While critical praise of the event in the *New York Times* and the *Village Voice* helped validate the genre, the sold-out attendance proved that there was a significant market for hip hop performance downtown. After the Ritz event, the more popular uptown acts such as Kurtis Blow, Grandmaster Flash and the Furious Five, and the Funky 4+1 began performing primarily at large Manhattan live music venues. A step up from entertaining clubbers at general hip hop spectacles, these acts eventually received headline billing and drew crowds on their own merits.

As illustrated by the coverage of the Ritz Rap Party, the new downtown location brought hip hop performance into direct contact with some of the world's most important music journalists. These writers played a significant role in the dissemination of hip hop downtown and around the United States. Before the Ritz Rap Party, few words about rap music had appeared in major New York publications. Christgau began reviewing twelve-inch singles for the first time in his "Consumer Guide" in the 25–31 March 1981 issue of the *Village Voice*. Since there were still no hip hop LPs at this point, sans Kurtis Blow's debut, the exclusion of twelve-inch singles also meant the absence of hip hop recordings from his column. Christgau, after explaining his decision to expand his criteria for reviewing material, made good on his claim that he "had a lot of catching up to do" by reviewing Afrika Bambaataa, Kurtis Blow, Funky 4+1, Grandmaster Flash and the Furious Five, and the Treacherous Three in the same issue (Christgau 1981). Christgau at the *Voice* and Palmer at the *New York Times* regularly reviewed and recommended hip hop recordings and performances throughout the years of the uptown-downtown nexus. The tireless efforts of New York music writers created interest in and lent legitimacy to hip hop when its popularity and validity as an art form had not yet been solidified.

"Tricked into Yelling 'Ho!'": The Rock Audience

The advocacy of rock musicians was another important factor in the rise of hip hop in lower Manhattan. In the spirit of Blondie's patronage of Fab 5 Freddy and Funky 4+1, the Clash, Malcolm McLaren, and other punks and new wavers exposed hip hop to new audiences. Delivering the keynote address at the 1982 New Music Seminar, McLaren devoted the majority of his speech to hip hop music. Familiar with the concepts and language of the industry, McLaren declared hip hop "the most rootsy folk music around" and "the only music that's coming out of New York City which tapped and directly related to the guy in the streets." He concluded that, "if Elvis Presley was that in the '50s, then Afrika Bambaataa is that for the '80s" (Hager 1982). While McLaren's rhetoric helped initiate the dialogue about hip hop as urban American folk culture, his bold comparison to Elvis

Presley no doubt left dollar signs in the eyes of the record industry. He himself attempted to capitalize on the phenomenon, releasing his own rap hit, "Buffalo Gals," in 1982.

After hearing "Rapper's Delight" and other early rap singles while visiting New York, the Clash included a rap in "The Magnificent Seven" on their *Sandinista!* album. Futura 2000 designed their stage sets, painted live backdrops at their concerts, designed their *Combat Rock* album cover, and rapped on "Overpowered by Funk" and "The Escapades of Futura 2000." While the Clash's fans accepted graffiti as a stage backdrop and an occasional rap in a song, it remained unclear as to how they would react to a live hip hop act.

This marriage of punk and rap in a live setting was tested at the Clash's 1981 infamous eighteen-night stand at Bond's International Casino in Times Square. Each night the band invited their favorite acts to play unbilled support slots. Opening the show on the first night of the engagement, Grandmaster Flash and the Furious Five—despite being adorned to the hilt in flamboyant stage attire— failed to win over the rock audience with their good-time anthems and choreographed dance moves. The band was shouted down and driven off-stage by a "hail of paper cups." Hoping to inspire a better reception from the dressed-down crowd, Flash and the Five appeared the next night low-key street attire. Despite the wardrobe modification, the group was again driven offstage by shouts and paper cups (Hill 1981).

While the fate of the Grandmaster Flash shows suggested that rap might never catch on with rock audiences, five days later the Treacherous Three's opening slot performance proved that punks could accept hip hop if it was presented differently. Punk rock DJ Pearl Harbor, who also was the "unofficial emcee" of the shows, "reminded the audience that all support acts were 'friends of the Clash.'" She helped create an atmosphere for the music by playing familiar Motown singles. The Treacherous Three then took the stage rapping about the Clash and began to engage the crowd in audience participation. In the words of *Village Voice* journalist Michael Hill, "the audience didn't have time to get mad ... because they had been tricked into yelling, 'Ho!'" (Hill 1981).

This anecdote illustrates how hip hop's crossover success required more than merely placing the acts in front of white rock audiences—the young genre needed to be effectively placed in the right context. The Treacherous Three also altered the content of their performance to win the crowd's acceptance. Rapping about the Clash seemed to have succeeded more than Grandmaster Flash's change of attire. Both bands' attempts to modify their presentation are evidence that hip hop modified its practices to adapt to the new environments and audiences. Recorded at the request of Sylvia Robinson, "The Message," Grandmaster Flash and the Furious Five's first sociopolitical song, appeared less than a year after their engagement with the politically conscious Clash. The Furious Five, like the Clash, were now talking about social issues instead of astrological signs and birthdays. The arrival of "The Message" resulted in a number of feature articles by white writers praising the Five's new social consciousness.[12]

Bambaataa: Beyond the Rap Map

A Bronx native and one of the founding fathers of hip hop, Afrika Bambaataa had been placing rock records in a context that hip hop audiences could appreciate since the 1970s. Bambaataa, "the Master of Records," also had both the knowledge and the vinyl to appeal to a downtown audience. His experiments with the fusion of rap, rock, funk, electronic music, and other genres had appeal across cultural lines, creating a soundtrack that served as a force that united downtown's increasingly diverse audiences under one groove on a weekly basis. A 1982 *Village Voice* feature recounts the story of Bambaataa's first appearance downtown:

> Bambaataa was greatly impressed, not only by the enthusiasm and energy of the crowd, but by their appreciative response to "Zulu Nation Throwdown" … What Bambaataa did was to go into the studio and immediately begin work on a new record, one that would appeal to the new wave crowd as well as the hip-hoppers. (Hager 1982)

The record, Afrika Bambaataa and Soul Sonic Force's "Planet Rock," illustrates the potential of cultural hybridity to birth unique forms. Much more than the material realization of Fab 5 Freddy's shuttling back and forth between the north and south poles of New York, "Planet Rock" was the next step forward. While "Rapture" or Tom Tom Club's "Wordy Rappinghood" are excellent illustrations of hip hop's early influence on downtown music, and "Genius Rap" and "It's Nasty" show downtown's influence on the uptown sound, none of these examples sufficiently departs from its initial genre to create something entirely new. The stark distinction between "Planet Rock" and its predecessors not only establishes the recording as the ultimate sonic relic of the uptown-downtown nexus, but also marks it as the climax of this narrative.

More than a rap record attempting to appeal to a rock audience or a rock record attempting to appeal to a rap audience, "Planet Rock" is its own animal. While the recording contains hip hop elements such as MCing and DJing, the vocoder singing, synthesizers, and drum machines place the song somewhere between the futuristic 1970s rock and funk music of Kraftwerk and Parliament. Here the Soul Sonic Force debuts their new "MC popping" technique in which the rappers cut phrases with abrupt pauses and overlaps. In an era in which most rap records featured funk bands instead of DJs, Bambaataa provides a soundscape comprised exclusively of electronic instruments and turntables. Additionally, the primary sample in the song, from Kraftwerk's "Trans Europe Express," is also completely synthetic.

"Planet Rock" is also unique in its creative employment of cutting-edge sound technologies. The beat, emanating from the just-released Roland TR-808 drum machine, has a highly artificial tone with an ultra-low bottom and a bright, thin snare sound. After "Planet Rock," the device immediately became a standard in rap, freestyle, and dance-pop in general. John Robie's artful programming and layering of synthesizer sounds also contributes to the piece's futuristic feel. When Tom Silverman requested "a polyphonic orchestral hit on the studio's Fairlight keyboard," Robie obliged, resulting in what David Toop describes as an effect that "combined the qualities of a Grandmaster Flash scratch, amplified to monstrous bandwidth, with the science-fiction suggestion of ten orchestras, all playing in perfect synchronization" (Toop 2000: 99). Imitations of this sound can also be found on countless club hits of various genres in the years that immediately followed.

Uptown and Downtown: Random Points in an Expanding Universe

After the climax of "Planet Rock" in early 1982, hip hop, originating in the Bronx and making a stop in lower Manhattan, had enveloped the globe by 1983. The successful European "Roxy Tour," a package featuring Bambaataa, Rock Steady Crew, Fab 5 Freddy, and the McDonald's Double Dutch Girls, spread hip hop to new international and corporate levels in November 1982 (Light 1999: 49-50). During the tour, the Rock Steady Crew accepted Queen Elizabeth's invitation to dance for her at the Royal Variety Performance (Backspin Productions 2004). In addition to breaking's introduction to a mass audience in *Flashdance* and hip hop's film debut in *Wild Style,* and the impending PBS broadcast of *Style Wars, Beat Street,* the first in a number of major studio hip hop films, was already in production. Most importantly, 1983 saw the release of Run DMC's first single "It's Like That" backed with "Sucker MCs" and the Beastie Boys' hip hop-informed "Cooky Puss." By 1983, hip hop, no longer a grassroots movement, was developing an infrastructure for what would become a multibillion dollar industry.

Springboarding their careers from the Roxy, the Danceteria, and other downtown venues, Run DMC, the Beastie Boys, and LL Cool J were among the new generation of rap artists whose sounds developed while hip hop's home base was Manhattan. All were managed by Queens concert promoter/manager Russell Simmons' Rush Productions. Run DMC, signed to Profile Records, was the first to streamline hip hop sound, fashion, and performance aesthetics. Replacing disco beats with hard rock beats, flamboyant stage attire with basic street attire, and dance routines with a static "b-boy stance," Run DMC became the biggest hip hop act of their time. Simmons and downtown punk rock producer/musician Rick Rubin met in 1984 and became partners in Rubin's Def Jam label (Light 1999: 156). Rather than "produced by Rick Rubin," LL Cool J's 1985 debut album, *Radio*, contained the credit "reduced by Rick Rubin." Further articulating the stripped-down rock-based sound being developed by Run DMC, *Radio*, followed in 1986 by the Beastie Boys' *License to Ill*, cemented new standards for the hip hop sound. While Rush's artists had driven rap deep into the pop and R&B charts by 1986, in the process they also displaced Grandmaster Flash and the Furious Five, Afrika Bambaataa and Soul Sonic Force, and the other original Bronx DJs and MCs at the forefront of the hip hop movement. Similarly, as new wave and punk styles exemplified by now-defunct bands such as Blondie and the Clash disappeared from the popular music charts, hip hop entered the Top 40 not only via Def Jam, but also through dance pop and other styles influenced by the genre.[13]

The final step in the integration of uptown and downtown aesthetics, the Run DMC/Def Jam aesthetic left no need for an uptown-downtown alliance, largely through the efforts of artists such as Bambaataa to create a hybrid sound that would appeal to both audiences. By 1985, hip hop music, its producers, its stars, and its audiences were from all parts of New York. None of Rush's major acts were Bronx-based.[14] The Bronx and Harlem were now only two of many hip hop locations. Just as uptown was no longer equated with hip hop, downtown was no longer associated with its new crossover audience. Hip hop was now becoming a part of multiracial life from the suburbs to the inner cities, from coast to coast, and across oceans. The music was now a national phenomenon, no longer tied to Manhattan.

As for how hip hop became mass culture, downtown was clearly a pivotal point in the genre's voyage to the stratosphere. While Fab 5 Freddy and other members of downtown's art and music scenes gave rap a new cultural context and geographic location, the skill and creativity of the practitioners of the powerful new musical genre were ultimately responsible for its success. The story of hip hop's journey downtown illustrates music's ability to transcend boundaries of geography, race, ethnicity, class, and culture. The uptown-downtown nexus also exhibits the way in which a few individuals can bring previously isolated groups of people together and, in the process, permanently change the world.

Notes

1. The death of disco had an important effect on the pop scene—especially in radio, where backpedaling programmers were shying away from black records of any kind in an effort to stay as far from the "disco" tag as possible. By the time "Rapper's Delight" was

released in 1979, these programmers were deep into the process of segregating the airwaves to a degree not seen since the pre-rock era. While in a typical week in the first half of 1979 nearly fifty percent of the records on *Billboard*'s pop singles chart could also be found on the R&B chart, by the first half of 1980 that number had dropped to twenty-one percent, and by the end of 1982 the crossover percentage was at a rock-era low of seventeen percent. In the extreme, October 1982 saw a three-week period during which not one record by an African American could be found in the Top 20 on *Billboard*'s pop singles or albums charts—a polarization that had not occurred since the 1940s (Light 1999: 26-27).

2. It is important to note that both the uptown hip hop and the downtown art scenes were not homogeneous in terms of race, ethnicity, gender, or class. But when hip hop went downtown, it broadened the variety of people and the cultural influences that they brought along with them.

3. "Comprised of disc jockeys (DJs/turntablists), emcees (MCs), breakdancers (b-boys and b-girls), and graffiti writers (aerosol artists)—commonly referred to as its four elements—hip-hop further encompasses what its adherents describe as an attitude rendered in the form of stylized dress, language, and gestures associated with urban street culture" (Keyes 2002: 1).

4. "In like the very late '70s and early '80s. Everything died down in Hip-Hop and we [Afrika Bambaataa and the Jazzy Five] went from playing in front of thousands of people at the parties—we found ourselves now playing for like 25 people! It happened for about a year and a half" (Ivory and Paul S. 2004). "Then our audience was getting older. I was wondering where my core audience was going. They wanted to move on and wear a dress or a suit" (Chang 2004).

5. "King Tim III (Personality Jock)" and "Rapper's Delight," which contain rhyming over funk jams, are typically considered the first two rap records (Keyes 2002: 70; Light 1999: 26; Fricke and Ahearn 2002: 177). As this paper is not concerned with the debate about what constitutes rap, I'll agree with the experts for the moment.

6. "Rapper's Delight," reaching #4 on the R&B chart and #36 on the Pop chart, sold over two million copies.

7. It is also important to note that, unlike the homemade cassettes, rap's initial recordings featured live bands instead of turntablists behind the rappers. Accordingly, those who heard these songs on the radio were not necessarily prepared for live hip hop music.

8. "Cassette tapes used to be our albums before anybody recorded what they called rap records. People started hearing all this rapping coming out of boxes. When they heard the tapes down in the Village they wanted to know, 'Who's this black DJ who's playing all this rock and new wave up in the Bronx'" (Toop 2000: 132).

9. Fab 5 Freddy: "At that time people weren't seeing all these different elements as one thing, you know? It was like people doing graffiti were just doing graffiti. Rapping people were rapping. The break-dance scene would go on at hip-hop parties, but it was pretty much like a Latin thing, so there were Latin clubs that would happen where break-dancing would go on. So I had this idea to bring these things together" (Fricke and Ahearn 2002: 290).

10. A parody of Studio 54, the Mudd Club initially had a velvet rope and selected patrons based on their physical appearance. Patrons pulling up in limousines were often forced to wait as poor downtown artists were admitted.

11. Afrika Bambaataa: "I ended up in Negril with Michael Holman and Lady Blue. Thursday nights down there became one of the biggest nights downtown. Then it got too big for Negril. One time the fire marshals closed the whole place down so we moved it to

Danceteria. Finally, we made home at The Roxy. It started slow building at The Roxy, and now Friday nights it's always 3000, 4000. Then it became a big commercial thing." (Toop 2000: 133).

12. Not only did the *Village Voice* praise "The Message" (Aletti 1982) but also both Robert Palmer and John Rockwell in completely separate articles wrote pieces in the *New York Times* about the song. Palmer wrote, "'The Message' has radically expanded the horizons of rap" (Palmer 1981b: 20). Rockwell concluded that "sometimes tension sparks creativity, too, and with 'The Message' that seems to have happened to Grandmaster Flash and the Furious Five" (Rockwell 1982).

13. The new hip hop-influenced style of dance pop is best exemplified by Bronx-born DJ Jellybean Benitez's production on Madonna's multi-platinum self-titled debut album. The beats for this style of music relied heavily on the feature of early hip hop that Def Jam left on the cutting room floor—the disco beat. The electronic instrumentation places it in the post-"Planet Rock" category. On a final note, Madonna herself was a regular at the Roxy's "Wheels of Steel" and took the Beastie Boys on her first arena tour.

14. Run DMC (not on Def Jam) and LL Cool J were from Queens. The Beastie Boys and the Fat Boys were from Brooklyn.

References

Aletti, Vince. 1981. "Golden Voices and Hearts of Steel." *Village Voice*, 18-24 March: 57.
———. 1982. "Furious." *Village Voice*, 20-26 July: 63.
"Archive Interviews: Arthur Baker." 1999. *Djhistory.com*.
    http://www.djhistory.com/books/archiveInterviewDisplay.php?interview_id=8 (accessed 4 October 2004).
"Archive Interviews: Charlie Ahearn." 2001. *Djhistory.com*.
    http://www.djhistory.com/books/archiveInterviewDisplay.php?interview_id=13 (accessed 4 October 2004).
Austin, Joe. 2001. *Taking the Train: How Graffiti Art Became an Urban Crisis in New York City*. New York: Columbia University Press.
Banes, Sally. 1981. "Breaking is Hard to Do." *Village Voice*, 22-28 April: 31-33.
Backspin Productions. 2004. "The Legendary Rock Steady Crew: Biography."
    http://rocksteadycrew.com (accessed 4 October 2004).
Brewster, Bill, and Frank Broughton. 2000. *Last Night a DJ Saved My Life: The History of the Disc Jockey*. New York: Grove Press.
Chalfant, Henry, and Martha Cooper. 1984. *Subway Art*. New York: Holt, Rinehart and Winston.
Chang, Jeff. 2004. "1982: The Year the Planet Rocked."
    http://www.kingtubbis.com/ex2/herc.html (accessed 4 October 2004).
Christgau, Robert. 1981. "Christgau's Consumer Guide." *Village Voice*, 25-31 March: 90.
Frank, Peter, and Michael McKinzie. 1987. *New, Used & Improved*. New York: Abeville Press.
Fricke, Jim, and Charlie Ahearn. 2002. *Yes Yes Y'all: The Experience Music Project Oral History of Hip-Hop's First Decade*. New York: Da Capo Press.
George, Nelson, Sally Banes, Susan Flinker, and Patty Romanowski. 1985. *Fresh: Hip Hop Don't Stop*. New York: Random House.

"Guide to the Fashion Moda Archive 1978-1993." 2003. Fales Library and Special Collections, New York University. http://dlib.nyu.edu:8083/falesead/servlet/SaxonServlet?source=/fashion.xml&style=/saxon01f2002.xsl&part=body (accessed 4 October 2004).

Hager, Steve. 1982. "Afrika Bambaataa's Hip Hop." *Village Voice,* 21-27 September: 69-73.

———. 1986. *Art After Midnight: The East Village Scene.* New York: St. Martin's Press.

Hill, Michael. 1981. "The Clash at the Clampdown." *Village Voice,* 10-16 September: 74.

Hoban, Phoebe. 1998. *Basquiat: A Quick Killing In Art.* New York: Viking.

Ivory and Paul S. (The P Brothers). n.d. "Interviews: Jazzy–Jazzy-Jay-Jay-Jay." *The Heavy Bronx Experience.* http://www.heavybronx.com/interviews/jazzyj.htm (accessed 4 October 2004).

Keller, Travis. 2004. "An Interview with Michael Diamond." *Buddyhead.* http://buddyhead.com/music/miked/ (accessed 4 October 2004).

Keyes, Cheryl. 2002. *Rap Music and Street Consciousness.* Urbana: University of Illinois Press.

"Kitchen Birthday Party" advertisement. 1981. *Village Voice,* 27 May-2 June: 70.

Light, Alan, ed. 1999. *The Vibe History of Hip Hop.* New York: Three Rivers Press.

Mudd Club advertisement. 1981. *Village Voice,* 8–14 April: 109.

Palmer, Robert. 1981a. "Pop: The Sugar Hill Gang." *New York Times,* 13 March: C23.

———. 1981b. "Pop/Jazz: 'The Message' Is That 'Rap' is Now King in Rock Clubs." *New York Times,* 3 September: C4.

"Patti Astor Interview." 2002. *@149th New York Cyber Bench.* http://www.at149st.com/astor.html (accessed 4 October 2004).

Quan, Jay. 2004. "Interview With Grandmixer DXT." *The Foundation: The Original School, 1975-1982,* 11 January. http://www.jayquan.com/dst.htm (accessed 4 October 2004).

Prasad, Anil. 1999. "Bill Laswell: Extending Energy and Experimentation." *Music Without Borders Innerviews,* 27 April. http://www.innerviews.org/inner/laswell.html (accessed 4 October 2004).

"Rap Records: Are They a Fad or Permanent?" 1980. *Billboard,* 16 February: 57-59.

"Ritz Rap Party" Advertisement. 1981. *Village Voice,* 4-10 March.

Rockwell, John. 1982. "Rap: The Furious Five." *New York Times,* 12 September: 84.

"Saturday Night Live Guests by Season." n.d. *Saturday-Night-Live.com.* http://www.saturday-night-live.com/snl/guestsbyseason.html (accessed 4 October 2004).

Simmons, Russell, with Nelson George. 2001. *Life and Def.* New York: Crown Publishers.

Toop, David. 2000. "Iron Needles of Death and a Piece of Wax." In *Modulations: A History of Electronic Music: Throbbing Words on Sound,* edited by Peter Shapiro, 88-107. New York: Caipirinha Productions, Inc.

Webster, Sally. 1996. "Fashion Moda: A Bronx Experience." http://ca80.lehman.cuny.edu/gallery/talkback/fmwebster.html (accessed 4 October 2004).

Discography/Filmography

Afrika Bambaataa and Soul Sonic Force. 1980. "Zulu Nation Throwdown" (12" single). Paul Winley Records 12x33-9.

———. 1982. "Planet Rock" (12" single). Tommy Boy 823.

Ahearn, Charlie, dir. 1979. *The Deadly Art of Survival*. CineFile Video.

———. 1982. *Wild Style*. Rhino Home Video.

Beastie Boys. 1983. "Cooky Puss" (12" single). Rat Cage Records MOTR 26.

Blondie. 1980. "Rapture." On *Autoamerican*. Chrysalis 1290.

Blow, Kurtis. "Christmas Rappin'" (12" single). Mercury BLOW 1312.

Chalfant, Henry, and Tony Silver, producers. 1983. *Style Wars*. Reissued in 2003 on DVD by Plexifilm.

The Clash. 1980. "Magnificent Seven." On *Sandinista!* Epic E3X-37037.

———. 1982. "Overpowered by Funk." On *Combat Rock*. Epic 37689.

———, with Futura 2000. 1983. "The Escapades of Futura 2000" (12" single). Celluloid 104.

Dr. Jeckyll and Mr. Hyde. 1981. "Genius Rap" (12" single). Profile Records 7004.

Fatback Band. "King Tim III (Personality Jock)." On *XII*. IMS 16723.

Funky 4+1 More. 1979. "Rappin' And Rocking The House" (12" single). Enjoy Records 6000.

Grandmaster Flash and the Furious Five. 1981. "It's Nasty" (12" single). Sugar Hill 569.

Hancock, Herbie. 1983. "Rockit." On *Future Shock*. Columbia Records 38814.

McLaren, Malcolm, and the World Famous Supreme Team. 1982. "Buffalo Gals" (12" single). Charisma MALC 1–12.

Run DMC. 1983. "It's Like That" / "Sucker MCs" (12" single). Profile Records 7019A.

Spoonie Gee. 1979. "Spoonin Rap" (12" single). Sound Of New York 708.

Sugarhill Gang. 1979. "Rapper's Delight" (12" single). Sugar Hill Records 542.

Tom Tom Club. 1981. "Genius of Love" and "Wordy Rappinghood." On *Tom Tom Club*. Sire SRK/XM5S 3628.

Gender Dynamics in the Film *Anne B. Real*

STEPHANIE JENSEN-MOULTON

Introduction: Putting her Raps on a New Map

> *I flow with the riddle that's golden and little, but large in our hearts.*
> *I'm provoked but the knowledge entice us,*
> *I'm broke but this knowledge is priceless,*
> *Consider this an amazing youth, that will blaze the truth and*
>   *raise the roof*
> *With nothing but power.*
>   —"This is Dedicated" from *Anne B. Real*

In the midst of a white, middle-class feminist scholarship that virtually ignored their existence, women of color put themselves on the map by pointing out the trouble with the map itself. In the words of Chandra Talpade Mohanty, "feminist struggles are waged on at least two simultaneous, interconnected levels: an ideological, discursive level which addresses questions of representation (womanhood/femininity), and a material, experiential daily-life level which focuses on the micropolitics of work, home, family, sexuality, etc." (Mohanty [1991] 2003: 21). Mohanty asserts that women who live in the geographical Third World are not necessarily "Third World women," and that women who live in First World nations may in reality live in the Third World. As problematic as the term "Third World" may be, women of color who wrote critiques of second wave feminism in the 1980s and 1990s found the term useful for establishing a discursive feminist space in which they could compose cultural critiques.

This chapter will explore how film texts can serve as cultural maps that require us, as viewer-participants, to negotiate multiple levels of feminist struggle, and to locate what we see and hear according to our own ideologies and experiences of daily life. One text that challenges the literal and discursive boundaries of the Third World is the 2002 independent film *Anne B. Real*, directed by Lisa France. In the movie, a young Afro-Latina named Cynthia struggles to build her identity as an MC in the Morningside Heights section of New York City. France's film focuses exclusively on this young woman's experience, thereby creating a complex female character, as opposed to the stereotypical objectified, hypersexualized female figures present in many rap movies. Despite Cynthia's tumultuous and trauma-filled ghetto life, she is able to find a voice through the medium of hip hop, and specifically in the primarily masculine space of an MC battle.

This family-friendly film contains no profanity, no nudity, and only mild violence.[1] France feminizes rap and the ghetto for broad consumption, and the music featured in her film both challenges and reinscribes gendered notions about women in the New York City hip hop scene. The contradictory nature of the film's depiction of a female rapper's struggle is typical of the type of neo-feminism espoused by many women in the late 1990s and in the current historical moment. I contend that the music in *Anne B. Real* weakens Cynthia where the plot would intend to strengthen her. If gender is, in Suzanne Cusick's words, "a system of assigning social roles, power and prestige that is sustained by a vast web of metaphors and cultural practices commonly associated with 'the masculine' or 'the feminine'" (Cusick 1999: 475), Cynthia's raps and her status as composer/performer complicate these societal boundaries by destabilizing preconceptions about race and gender in hip hop. Similarly, the soundtrack functions as a multiple signifier for the visual aspects of the piece, contributing to a breakdown of the aural/visual binary so important in feminist analyses of film. Thus, female rappers' big screen personae, when examined through the lens of feminist theory, create a myth of female hip hop culture in post-9/11 New York City.

Seeing Aurally

> *You need to stop frontin, you sneakin, you caught,*
> *You don't be rhymin you be speakin my thoughts.*
> —"They Call Me Real" from *Anne B. Real*

In *Anne B. Real*, Cynthia's brother Juan represents the sole support for his extended family of women, all living in one small apartment in Morningside Heights. From the start, Cynthia's identity has been formed by the male influences in her life: her father, a teacher, admonished her always to trust her older brother. Cynthia and Juan's father recently died (the film does not tell us how or why), and his voice is often heard as a voiceover in Cynthia's thoughts. In a black-and-white flashback, a technique used throughout the film, Cynthia's dad gives her a copy of *Anne Frank: The Diary of a Young Girl* ([1952] 1993). Cynthia spends a good portion of her screen time reading the book, and through a voice-over we hear her silently reading in a kind of embryonic finding of the personal voice. From *Anne Frank* Cynthia takes her rapper name, Annie B. Real. Her choice of MC name carries special significance not only because of her struggle for truth and authenticity in the film, but also because it enables Cynthia to carry a distinctly female persona onto the hip hop stage.

In her essay "Film as Ethnography; or, Translation between Cultures in the Postcolonial World," Rey Chow utilizes the term "to-be-looked-at-ness" to signify "what constitutes not only the spectacle but the very way vision is organized; the state of being looked at ... is built into the way we look" (Chow 1995: 179). It is possible to speak of a to-be-*listened*-to-ness that plays an equally important role in film study, yet is often neglected in feminist analyses of film texts. While visual image is crucial in film, it seems inconceivable that modern films with sound-tracks could be considered theoretically without analysis of the music chosen to carry the audience member through the spectacle. Just as "observer" and "observed" indicate a structure of power, aural and visual in film always already form a hierarchy. Even the terms "film" and "soundtrack" imply that the latter is simply an additive, while the former is somehow more complete: a subject that is grounded in images. When listening is examined as an essential part of viewing, the approach to visual "otherness" alters, and aural transmission of culture begins. In this way, every film produced—documentary, low-budget feature, or block-buster hit—can be considered a type of ethnography. "To-be-listened-to-ness" is an act of cross-cultural representation that locates meaning in what is seen *through* what is heard, allowing new, multidimensional cartographies of feminism to take form.

The score composed specifically for *Anne B. Real* by Dean Parker (as opposed to the compiled, pre-existent popular music utilized in the film[2]) has mostly classical music features, with some jazz influence. Guthrie Ramsey employs the terms "diagetic" and "nondiagetic" to describe two types of film music. While diagetic music, also called source music, evokes the fictional world of the film and seems to emerge from within it, nondiagetic music functions outside of the narrative, yet serves it, as Ramsey states,

> by signaling emotional states, propelling dramatic action, depicting a geographi-cal location or time period, among other factors ... Another kind of musical address in film blends the diagetic and nondiagetic. Earle Hagen calls this type of film music source scoring. In source scoring the musical cue can start out as diagetic but then change over to nondiagetic. (Ramsey 2003: 172)

In the context of *Anne B. Real*, the use of diagetic and nondiagetic music employs and occasionally reverses Earle Hagen's definition of source scoring cited above. Two distinctly different film scores play off of one another in *Anne B. Real*, serving as mutual signifiers of both internal and external location. The original raps writ-ten for the film play much the same role as the classical score: to illuminate and reveal Cynthia's inner life and personal voice. Conversely, the raps selected from the vast repertory of hip hop albums in circulation at the time tend to elucidate the external, such as events in Juan's life and the presence of violence in Cynthia's everyday world. Thus, the soundtrack of *Anne B. Real* is as filled with as many contradictions as Cynthia's character. Hip hop cannot be separated completely from the Western art music score, and this blending of styles weakens Cynthia's voice as a rapper.

In the opening sequence of the film, a small chamber ensemble (eight string players, flute, oboe, bassoon, and piano) plays the sustained G major triad shown in Example 1 with plenty of vibrato, while the lower strings play a recurrent upward motive. The sequences during which this motive or a related motive appears are the emotional keystones of the film; when we hear quotations from Anne Frank's diary in Cynthia's voiceover, this rising string motive recurs. Victoria Johnson suggests that in a traditional model,

> film music exists to enhance the purported and desired seamlessness of the narrative ... The conventional score is typically characterized by several elements, including a strong orientation to nineteenth-century European Romanticism, which prioritizes melody, lush sound, and full orchestration, and a frequent reliance on leitmotifs, which are variously associated with specific themes or characters. (Johnson 1993-1994:18)

By this definition, *Anne B. Real*'s composed score would certainly fall into the category of "traditional film music." Yet, when juxtaposed with original rap sequences and pre-existing hip hop music, the orchestral moments in *Anne B. Real* might be understood as aural clues to a cross-historical relationship: Cynthia's connection to Anne Frank. Nevertheless, listeners may identify with one, both, or neither of the musical styles employed in the film, and this identification stratifies viewers in spite of the visual text. One viewer might identify with the picture on the screen, but not with the classical music she hears; another might identify with both the rap and classical scores. Thus, film viewers must reexamine their cultural positionality as film listeners.

Perhaps the classical score is also meant to form a counterpoint with the rap music so prevalent in the soundtrack. Just as Annie B. Real's raps and the text of *Anne Frank* are interwoven but never mixed in the film, so functions the art music score alongside the popular music selections. The classical score appears to serve as a bridge connecting Anne Frank's experience to Cynthia's—two manifestations of Third World women's experiences outside of the geographic Third World—and the visual text adds yet another dimension. The film's opening shot focuses on a section of razor wire and a watchtower-like structure above train tracks. This clear allusion to Nazi concentration camps (and thereby to Anne Frank's writings) clarifies musical meaning for the viewer-listener. The score, grounded in a European, classical aesthetic, evokes early twentieth-century Europe. It is the only moment in the film when classical and rap music overlap, and we hear and see Cynthia rapping unsuccessfully in front of her bathroom mirror to the tune of a mournful cello. Thus, the first sound we hear in this film text about a female rapper is the rising string motive shown in Example 1 and rhymes that die on her lips as she attempts them, shaking her head in discouragement. When contrasted with the first appearance of Eminem in Curtis Hanson's 2002 film *8 Mile,* which is underscored by persistent eighth-note attacks from Mobb Deep's "Shook Ones Pt. II" on Eminem's discman, Cynthia is immediately heard *and* seen as subordinate in the power structure of hip hop narratives.

Example 1. Recurrent upward motive in unison celli and basses, with the piano line in the treble. From the original score of *Anne B. Real,* composed by Dean Parker.

"Lose Yourself": Erasing Identity in Hip-Hop Culture

He can read my writing but he sho' can't read my mind.
—Zora Neale Hurston, *Mules and Men*

The starring role in *Anne B. Real* is played by rapper JNYCE, or Janice Richardson. It is curious that she never freestyles or participates in the creation of Cynthia's on-screen raps; rather, JNYCE performs the raps written by Luis Moro and Canadian rapper Verse, which complicates the audience's perception of JNYCE (and Cynthia) as a real MC. The other female artists on the soundtrack (listed in the Appendix) are not rappers at all, but are R&B or pop singers. By using a pop song (Paula Cole's "Be Somebody") in the film to underscore one of Cynthia's important soliloquy walks through her neighborhood, and by framing it as the featured music from the movie, Cynthia's raps are subsumed before they are even heard. By contrast, in *8 Mile,* Eminem's rapping skills are heard throughout the film, and in the final credits "Lose Yourself" is heard in full. The *8 Mile* DVD features a music video entitled "Superman" which represents misogynistic gangsta rap, replete with images of barely clothed women all trying to participate in an orgiastic video fantasy with Eminem. In a scene which returns repeatedly in the video, Eminem is center screen while at least thirty women in G strings writhe amongst each other, all trying to access the oversexed Eminem. His persona, though modeled in the film as a defender of gay rights and the ideal older brother, shines through more effectively in the video, perhaps, than in the cinematic depiction of his life.

At this juncture, one must begin to problematize the suspension of disbelief in the film. In reality, none of Cynthia's rhymes was actually composed by a woman, though we see her performing them throughout the film. None of the music composed specifically for *Anne B. Real* had any female authorship, though several raps by women are utilized on the soundtrack. This complicates Cynthia's status as rapper-composer: on one level, we hear and see Cynthia rapping; on another, we understand that Cynthia is merely a fictional character played by Janice Richardson. How, then, can we as viewers reconcile JNYCE, playing Cynthia yet rapping compositions by men, with a character such as Bunny Rabbit in *8 Mile*? Rabbit's rhymes, all composed by Eminem for Eminem, lend authenticity not only to the character we see on screen, but also to Eminem himself. Why could not *Anne B. Real*'s producers entrust the creation of raps for the film to a real female rapper? Is this "a real rapper here" as Cynthia states at the beginning of her MC battle with Deuce? The only rap that is heard in its entirety in *Anne B. Real* is the one Cynthia performs in the ultimate scene of the movie during her MC battle with Deuce. A kind of acquisition of Deuce's voice occurs when Cynthia begins to rhyme in unison with him. Then the rap "They Call Me Real" establishes Cynthia's identity as the true writer of these rhymes. She can freestyle, whereas Deuce cannot. Because Cynthia has uncovered the truth about Deuce's theft and has confronted him publicly, he loses the battle, and is booed off the stage by a notably multiracial audience.

Racial dynamics present in *Anne B. Real* also complicate Cynthia's worldview. Director Lisa France comments on the intentionality of the "Latin Rainbow" represented in her film. She states: "I think America, particularly inner-city America, has become a big melting pot. You really have no idea who is what anymore. In my building there are families that do not look like each other, but they are blood related, first generation relatives. I wanted to show this shift in race ... We are going to eventually become so mixed up that no one will know what anyone is. I actually think this is part of nature's grand plan."[3] By viewing races as simply melded in the film, France succeeds in the erasure of racial identity for Cynthia. She is not permitted to acknowledge both her Black and her Hispanic roots, but is viewed primarily as Black in the film. She never speaks Spanish, though she lives in a house where Spanish is the first language. Her sister, more intimately involved in this household, speaks both Spanish and English in the film, while her mother speaks only some English and mostly Spanish. Both Cynthia's brother and sister were cast as very light-skinned. Cynthia, the darkest skinned in her family, forms her identity through what much scholarship considers to be a primarily Black, male medium. Additionally, her Blackness is emphasized by the light-skinned actors cast as her close friends. Only Jerome, the boy drug dealer murdered by Juan, is visually and aurally representative of the expected hip hop participant.

Jerome lives alone in a tiny room decorated with graffiti and containing only a bed, mirror, chest of drawers and set of turntables, and his sequences as drug dealer are underscored by rap music.

David Eng and Shinhee Han comment that "assimilation into mainstream culture for people of color still means adopting a set of dominant norms and ideals … often foreclosed to them" (Eng and Han 2003: 344). In a sense, Cynthia is claiming the identity of her father in assimilating herself into the hip hop scene instead of the private sphere of her mother and sister. Cynthia continually turns to the book given to her by her father. Like Anne Frank, who wrote because she had to write to survive, Cynthia represents the inner-city version of the organic intellectual, and this is reflected in her status as an autodidactic poet of rap.[4]

Reflexive Rap: Bathroom Feminism Hits Hip Hop

> *Hey yo I'm broke and I'm trapped, my hunger for money provoking my rap.*
> —"The Name is not Biblical" from *Anne B. Real*

> *A woman must have money and a room of her own if she is to write …*
> —Virginia Woolf, *A Room of One's Own*

Cynthia's brother Juan, thoroughly enmeshed in the public (though black market) sphere, is a drug addict in the film and has been selling Cynthia's rhymes to a rapper named Deuce for drug money. Juan has also been working as a hit man, and is responsible for the murder of one of Cynthia's friends, Jerome, early on in the film. Later, Juan is the indirect cause of the death of Cynthia's best friend Kitty, who is gunned down in the street by Juan's mob bosses. Juan and the other male characters in this film are static. There is no sense of change through the course of the film for Juan; he does not reform, but is arrested later in the film for armed assault. Deuce's character, also static, serves as a foil to Cynthia's bookish, reclusive persona. Deuce is presented as a caricature of the phony MC, and serves as a vehicle for the issue of authenticity in the film. He is all that Cynthia is not: he wears fashionable clothes and flaunts his talent, as well as his girlfriend, the aptly named Fendi. Deuce is seen outside the club Downtime (site of the eventual MC battle) handing his homemade CDs to the line of people waiting to get past the bouncer, while Cynthia is pictured in the private sphere surrounded by her female relatives. An excerpt of A Tribe Called Quest's track "Phony Rappers" comments upon Deuce's character in tandem with the visual text.

While Deuce struts his inauthentic stuff in clubs and recording studios, Cynthia spends much of her on-screen time in her bathroom, rapping in front of the mirror and holding a toothbrush as a mic. Her raps are not for public consumption. The thin curtain that serves as a bathroom door is utterly penetrable, and she is constantly interrupted by her sister Janet who accuses her of wasting space by holing up in her bedroom or the bathroom and mumbling. Janet is concerned about Cynthia, but does not take any action to help her. Janet, an unemployed, single mother living on welfare, summarizes her situation for the benefit of her ex-boyfriend in the film: "OK, you want to catch up? Here's the brief: I got pregnant, you left for college, my dad died, my sister's a freak, my brother's a drug addict, and we're on welfare. You all caught up now?" Janet mostly remains in the apartment; she is pictured folding laundry, sitting at a kitchen table, and in other clearly domestic poses. Janet never appears with a soundtrack. Her world lacks music, and the silence betrays the bleakness of her inner life.

The space of the bathroom, separate and enclosed, is essential, from a mental as well as a physical standpoint, to Cynthia's ability to compose. As Kristina Deffenbacher argues:

> In her psychic home, especially if not in her actual house, a woman writer seems to need four walls, a door, and perhaps some other decoys or other defenses outside that door. Such psychic architecture protects against certain contingencies— from family members making consuming demands or white men threatening to penetrate and colonize one's space. (Deffenbacher 2003: 106)

Throughout the film, we witness Cynthia's gradual composition of her rhymes in a plaid notebook (like the one Anne Frank reportedly used) and performance of them in private settings. Her loudmouth best friend Kitty finds her rapping in the school bathroom and encourages her to rap with some street rappers, but Cynthia is too shy and freezes under pressure. Kitty defends Cynthia at every turn; she is her voice before Cynthia finds hers as a rapper. It is only after Kitty's brutal murder on the street that Cynthia is able to fully enact her role as MC. All of the entries in Anne Frank's diary begin with "Dear Kitty." Because Frank felt as though she could not talk deeply with any friends at school, she invented Kitty as a literary confidante. Anne Frank's Kitty, though imaginary, functioned similarly to the twenty-first century incarnation of Kitty: a sometimes-exasperating though essential support system for female creativity.

Cynthia's dialogues with her reflected self often reveal her thoughts about friends', relatives', and teachers' opinions of her. It is in this context that Cynthia forms her identity as a female, a rapper, and a sister. Cynthia deals with the Western standard of beauty through the imagined picture of Jerome telling her she is ugly. She is assaulted by the imagined image of Juan repeating "You can't rap. Nobody wants to hear a girl on the mic. Why don't you get yourself a man? I need a nephew or something." Principal Davis (who in Cynthia's imagination enters this feminized, domestic space) admonishes that she needs therapy and is "average," nothing special. Though her raps are never underscored with mixes when she rehearses them in the mirror, we become familiar with the text and rhythm of her raps. This familiarity enables us to form the truth of Cynthia's identity as the real rapper, and to have explicit knowledge of Deuce's disregard for the unwritten moral codes of hip hop.[5] The mirror in this film text is symbolic not only of truth, but of the imaginary; it disembodies Cynthia, enacting a mind-body split that enables her to create.

In *Gender and the Musical Canon* (1993), Marcia Citron examines gendered differences in creativity. Many of the gender issues addressed by Citron in the context of Western, primarily European, female composers apply directly to Cynthia as she formulates an identity as rapper-composer. Citron argues that a Platonic—and later Cartesian—mind-body opposition exists between women's creativity (of the body) and men's creative impulses (of the mind). As Cynthia composes her rhymes in the quasi-privacy of her bedroom and bathroom, she is also mapping out a kind of feminist space where her writing will not be undervalued. In a sense, she is remapping her environment in order to create a private place reminiscent of that invoked in Woolf's *A Room of One's Own*. In the film, after Jerome's murder, Cynthia utilizes Jerome's apartment, rather than her home, to write and think; Jerome's room becomes her own through his illegal action and subsequent murder.[6]

When Cynthia's moral and social "choices" are questioned by her sister, Cynthia refuses to reenact Janet's struggle as a single mother. Thus, Cynthia's creative work is mental, while her sister's creativity remains in the patriarchally dominated realm of the procreative. As Cynthia's world becomes increasingly complex, her need to compose raps and reconcile these complexities with her inner life increases. Citron comments:

> composing may function for many female composers as a prime means of self-expression: not just a means of expression but as the main way to channel their inner selves into some tangible form. This might be different from the situation of males who compose. As the privileged gender in Western culture, men possess many more outlets for self-expression in addition to that of the art work. For women, composing per se has existed as more of a necessary activity. (1993: 58)

Cynthia's medium of expression, hip hop, likewise reflects the primary artistic practice of the people in her life and in her neighborhood. Thus, her need to compose naturally manifests itself in the form of rap lyrics and beats. The film's conflation of ideas and lines from *Anne Frank: The Diary of a Young Girl* also underscores this necessity of composition for women. For Frank, writing served as a survival tool in the midst of the unthinkable genocide of Jews during World

War II. More mentors than muses, Frank and her writing serve as cross-cultural creative guides for Cynthia as she negotiates her identity—and in some sense, her survival—in Morningside Heights. Yet, while Anne Frank wrote her diary entries with no idea that they would be read the world over, Cynthia has a vague notion that her brother is selling her work; her writing, therefore, is public, while she, the composer remains private. But she writes without the knowledge that her raps' composition will be attributed not to her, but to Deuce.

Whereas Deuce is a rapper, Cynthia is a composer of raps; she is the one who creates, but it is only in the end of the film that she is able to represent fully as performer. Clearly, she must be able to function as a performer in order to empower her status a creator, at least in this medium. Cynthia must actualize her rhymes in a physical performance before they are legitimate. Audience reception is crucial to the re-situation of truth in *Anne B. Real*, relating directly to Citron's discussions of female composers' professionalism. Whereas in Western art music, the composer is deemed a professional when work is published in a printed score, the moment of live hip hop performance becomes an essential site of composition for the MC. Yet, as Deuce produces "his" CDs for distribution among hip hop consumers, the quasi-publication of Cynthia's rhymes occurs under what is essentially a pen name and a privileged persona. Her rhymes are thus appropriated into a male paradigm of success. This transaction of sorts is facilitated by Cynthia's brother, the "head of household" in Cynthia's domestic world.

Similarly, in a subplot, we view Deuce in the studio recording Cynthia's raps. When asked to freestyle over the producer's new beat, Deuce cannot. He claims that it would be an insult to his artistry: "You wouldn't ask Bob Dylan to freestyle, would you?" That Deuce will not even attempt to create, but simply appropriates, is emblematic of the male appropriation of feminist texts. Citron notes: "Scores and other physical embodiments of music, including recordings, point up the materiality of Western canons and suggest canonic dependence on writing and the visual for preservation" (1993: 9). Deuce preserves Cynthia's rhymes on CD and in the studio, thereby legitimizing them to an audience of supposed hip hop aficionados. Were Deuce to perform the rhymes without physical distribution, his creative act would not have the power to subsume the physical, procreative female composition.

Cynthia cloisters herself in order to release her creative voice. In the bathroom, she confronts her fear that others think her foolish for trying to succeed in a man's world, the world of MCs. As she negotiates her identity as a rapper, Cynthia is also negotiating boundaries of race, class, and gender. She is not only poor, but also a female of color; her choice to remain in her own room and write is spurned by her sister and family. Cynthia's "confinement" in the film is not a physical, reproductive one, but instead represents her rebellion against, as Citron states, "the restrictive   traditions   concerning   women's   ability   to   create,   especially appropriation." The character of Cynthia can be read as

> attempt[ing] to reframe [these traditions] in feminist terms. For those who have composed, the negativity has had psychological consequences. In many cases it has led to ambivalence and doubt—or what has been termed an anxiety of authorship. The female composer may also have to commit a metaphorical murder of her depiction as a woman in previous works by men. This suggests texted works; in instrumental music more subtle codes may be operative. (1993: 9)

Issues of appropriation take on new meaning when viewed through the lens of hip hop critical writing. Much of the popular writing on rap refers to the necessity of "keeping it real" as opposed to commercializing and producing for the cultural and economic mainstream. Appropriation in Citron's context may refer to appropriation of women's creative work; in a hip hop context, Cynthia's rhymes are appropriated by Deuce for his own personal and monetary gain.

An additional way of understanding appropriation may refer to the appropriation of hip hop by mainstream culture as a symbolic tool: hip hop signifies Blackness to the mainstream. Even though countless artists from a wide array of cultural backgrounds perform within hip hop media, mainstream America, including academia, continues to view hip hop as a Black art form.[7] By utilizing hip hop as the backdrop for this particular story, Lisa France and the producers of *Anne B. Real* appropriate rap as a gendered, racialized music, but they also flip the script on this trope by examining the world of an Afro-Latina rapper. Principal Davis, however, admonishes Cynthia (through the imaginary window of the bathroom mirror): "And another thing: you are Black," as if to solidify through racial pigeonholing Cynthia's perception of her identity and to shut down any potential inspiration she might draw from it in her creative work. His imagined statement reveals still more about Cynthia's racial self-consciousness when one considers that the principal himself is Black.

The inner landscape that Cynthia enters via the bathroom mirror also alludes to a spiritual presence in the film, signaled by the icon of Mary found next to the bathroom mirror. Though Cynthia never actually goes to church in the film, allusions to religion, God, the Koran, the "man above" and his perfection, as well as a "golden riddle" (possibly alluding to the Golden Rule), all appear in Cynthia's raps. For example, the text of "This is Dedicated" contains many allusions to faith: "I stress my mistakes, put logic in God" and "I get my answers from the higher Koran, the G.D. with 'O' in the middle." These lyrics represent "conscious" rap, as opposed to the more explicit verses found in, for example, gangsta rap. On the DVD commentary track, France states that she wanted the film to be accessible to all audiences, from school age to elderly. Though veiled by France's assertion that the inclusion of profanity, nudity, and violence would narrow the scope of the audience, she clearly chose a screenplay centering on a female rapper as the vehicle for her "clean" aesthetic. Thus, Cynthia and her raps represent as pure, religious, and "feminine."

Citron's allusion to the psychological effects of composition and the subsequent anxieties about authorship are also manifested in *Anne B. Real* by Deuce. Because Cynthia grossly undervalued her rhymes, it was easy for her brother to obtain them. Her anxiety about presenting her raps in a public context also denotes her uneasy footing as a female rapper, effectively "murdering" the misogynist raps written by her male counterparts. Despite her construction as "feminine," she also contradictorily reads as a female rapper who rebels against the dominant norms and behaviors for female rappers, refusing to market herself by wearing sexy attire or performing titillating rhymes. Her "conscious" raps succeed in erasing the stereotypical female personae presented in gangsta raps, especially on the small screen.

Anne B. Real: A Post-9/11 Feminist Film Text?

> Yo we need to do some true building, before we lose more than two buildings.
> —"This is Dedicated" from *Anne B. Real*

> To read or watch the most powerful media, one would think that Bush's second-wave sexism is occurring in a post-feminist moment. And there's some truth to that.
> —Laura Flanders, "Feigning Feminism, Fueling Backlash"

Does the way music is used in *Anne B. Real* reinforce or weaken the film's possible status as a feminist text? Cynthia is encouraged to write, but not necessarily to rap, by the state, represented by a teacher at her high school. She is encouraged to rap by her friend Kitty, who is murdered. She is finally convinced to participate in the MC battle by her friend, Darius, who had revealed the truth about Deuce's acquisition of her rhymes. Does Cynthia ever exercise agency of her own? Women in poverty must create in unconventional ways—the act of finding a way to create is extraordinary. Though Cynthia's plight betrays inconsistencies characteristic of neo-feminism, the very existence of her creative work is subversive. The final scene in the film—the MC battle where Cynthia as Annie B. Real defeats (and debunks) Deuce—illustrates France's intention for Cynthia: to be read as a dynamic character who finds strength through composition and finally emerges as a "strong woman" morally, socially, and creatively.

In post-9/11 America, the image of a powerful woman is even less acceptable than before (Goldstein 2003; Flanders 2004). The desire for a type of neo-macho man who may be strong and wrong, but who can certainly do battle, has given rise to a type of neo-feminism which has been brewing since the mid-1990s. J. Ann Tickner writes in her feminist analysis of 9/11 that "the association of women with peace renders both women and peace as idealistic, utopian, and unrealistic; it is profoundly disempowering for both. And as long as peace remains associated with women, this may reinforce militarized masculinity" (2002: 334). Cynthia's emergent persona as a "conscious" rapper, one who encourages peace, prayer, and a reliance on higher spiritual powers for guidance, complicates the type of womanhood of which Tickner is writing. The conflation of Anne Frank's diary with a hip hop screenplay also reinforces the gendered binarism of peace and war.

Anne B. Real's use of both diagetic and nondiagetic music further complicates the neo-feminist argument. The film needs the art music score in order to create some element of the peace-bearing female, but also functions at a more basic level, to rally masculine support by the fronted strong-souled woman, one to whom the term "feminist" might sound distasteful. Joan Morgan asks, "Can you be a good feminist and admit out loud that there are things you kind of like about patriarchy?" (1999: 57).

> We need a feminism that possesses the same fundamental understanding held by any true student of hip-hop. Truth can't be found in the voice of any one rapper but in the juxtaposition of many. The keys that unlock the riches of contemporary black female identity lie not in choosing Latifah over Lil' Kim, or even Foxy Brown over Salt-N-Pepa. They lie at the magical intersection where those contrary voices meet—the juncture where "truth" is no longer black and white but subtle, intriguing shades of gray. (Morgan 1999: 62)

The neo-feminist, or "strong woman," wants feminism without the rough edges, on her own contradictory terms. She wants the man as protector and provider, but she wants her social and financial independence. She has no use for the label "feminist."

A film text such as *Anne B. Real* reinforces the "strong woman" trope in a hip hop context, both challenging (from the perspective of gender) and reinscribing (from the perspective of race) stereotypes about participants in hip hop culture and creating a myth of musical life in Morningside Heights. Cynthia's incomplete raps and underscoring with pop songs negate her status as a "real rapper," leaving viewers with a character who is simultaneously strong and weak. Yet *Anne B. Real* approaches issues of authenticity, gender, race, and power in novel ways, in spite of the myth it creates. In post-9/11 New York City, a neo-feminism wrought in discursive violence and fraught with contradiction is certainly better than no feminism at all.

Appendix. Pre-existent tracks used in the soundtrack of *Anne B. Real*. Female artists' names are noted with an asterisk.

"Feel The Girl" performed by Ms. Jade*
"Womanology" written and performed by KRS-One
"Drum Trip" performed by Rusted Root
"The Life" written and performed by Mystic*
"Be Somebody" performed by Paula Cole*
"Boy like Dat" performed by MC Lyte*
"I'm Leavin'" performed by Pigeon John
"Ghetto Birds" written and performed by Mystic*
"Phony Rappers" performed by A Tribe Called Quest
"Power" performed by End of the Weak
"Fallen Angels" performed by Mystic*
"Something is Going on Here" performed by Earthman and Shane Conry

Acknowledgments

My thanks to Ellie Hisama for her many insights, to Evan Rapport for helpful comments, and to Albert Jensen-Moulton for watching *Anne B. Real* with me again and again.

Notes

1. Note, however, that no rap is heard completely in the film, and complete versions of pre-existing rap tracks heard in *Anne B. Real* certainly do contain profanity and/or sexually explicit lyrics. The text for "Phony Rappers" is one example, as well as "Feel the Girl" by Ms. Jade, which was released in both explicit and clean versions.
2. See the Appendix.
3. http://www.mosaec.com/mosaec/film/film_lisafrance.htm (accessed 15 April 2004).
4. Eric Porter (2002) relates Antonio Gramsci's notion of the organic intellectual to jazz.
5. For a cogent discussion of ethics in hip hop production, see Schloss 2004, specifically Chapter 5, "Sampling Ethics."
6. A further connection to Woolf's contention that a woman must have not only a room but also money in order to create is the thick roll of cash under Jerome's bed, which Cynthia finds after Jerome's murder. She acknowledges the money, then replaces it under the bed, presumably for future use.
7. In an anecdotal example, a professor from another university assumed that all of the students in Professor Ellie Hisama's History/Theory/Criticism of Hip-Hop course at the CUNY Graduate Center were Black. See also Rose (1994: xiii); Flores (2000: 116); and Mitchell (2002).

References

Chow, Rey. 1995. "Film as Ethnography; or, Translation between Cultures in the Postcolonial World." In her *Primitive Passions*, 173-205. New York: Columbia University Press.

Citron, Marcia. 1993. *Gender and the Musical Canon*. Cambridge: Cambridge University Press.

Cusick, Suzanne G. 1999. "Gender, Musicology, and Feminism." In *Rethinking Music*, edited by Nicholas Cook and Mark Everist, 471-98. Oxford: Oxford University Press.

Deffenbacher, Kristina. 2003. "Woolf, Hurston, and the House of Self." In *Herspace: Women, Writing, and Solitude*, edited by Jo Malin and Victoria Boynton, 105-21. New York: The Haworth Press.

Eng, David L., and Shinhee Han. 2003. "A Dialogue on Racial Melancholia." In *Loss: The Politics of Mourning*, edited by David L. Eng and David Kazanjian, 343-71. Berkeley: University of California Press.

Flanders, Laura. 2004. "Introduction: Feigning Feminism, Fueling Backlash." In *The W Effect: Bush's War on Women*, edited by Laura Flanders, xi-xxi. New York: The Feminist Press.

Flores, Juan. 2000. *From Bomba to Hip-Hop: Puerto Rican Cultures and Latino Identity*. New York: Columbia University Press.

Frank, Anne. [1952] 1993. *Anne Frank: The Diary of a Young Girl*. Translated by B. M. Mooyaart-Doubleday. New York: Bantam Books.

Goldstein, Richard. 2003. "Neo-Macho Man: Pop Culture and Post-9/11 Politics." *The Nation*, 6 March: 16-20.

Hurston, Zora Neale. 1935. *Mules and Men*. New York: Harper and Row.

Johnson, Victoria E. 1993-1994. "Polyphony and Cultural Expression: Interpreting Musical Traditions in *Do the Right Thing*." *Film Quarterly* 47(Winter): 18-29.

Mitchell, Tony, ed. 2002. *Global Noise: Rap and Hip-Hop Outside the USA*. Middletown, CT: Wesleyan University Press.

Mohanty, Chandra Talpade. [1991] 2003. "Introduction: Cartographies of Struggle: Third World Women and the Politics of Feminism." In *Feminism Without Borders: Decolonizing Theory, Practicing Solidarity*, edited by Chandra Mohanty, 1-47. Durham: Duke University Press.

Morgan, Joan. 1999. *When Chickenheads Come Home to Roost: A Hip-Hop Feminist Breaks it Down*. New York: Simon and Schuster.

Porter, Eric. 2002. *What Is This Thing Called Jazz? African American Musicians as Artists, Critics, and Activists*. Berkeley: University of California Press.

Ramsey, Jr., Guthrie P. 2003. "Scoring a Black Nation: Music, Film, and Identity in the Age of Hip-Hop." In his *Race Music: Black Cultures from Bebop to Hip-Hop*, 163-89. Berkeley: University of California Press.

Rose, Tricia. 1994. *Black Noise: Rap Music and Black Culture in Contemporary America*. Middletown, CT: Wesleyan University Press.

Schloss, Joseph G. 2004. *Making Beats: The Art of Sample-Based Hip-Hop*. Middletown, CT: Wesleyan University Press.

Tickner, J. Ann. 2002. "Feminist Perspectives on 9/11." *International Studies Perspectives* 3: 333-50.

Woolf, Virginia. [1929] 1989. *A Room of One's Own*. San Diego: Harcourt Brace.

Discography/Filmography

France, Lisa. 2002. *Anne B. Real.* Screen Media Films. DVD.

Hanson, Curtis, dir. 2003. *8 Mile.* Universal Pictures and Imagine Entertainment. DVD.

KRS-One. 2002. "Womanology." On *Prophets vs. Profits.* Phantom B00006JOUG.

Ms. Jade. 2002. "Feel the Girl." On *Girl Interrupted.* Interscope Records 493442.

Paula Cole. 1999. "Be Somebody." On *Amen.* Warner Brothers 47490.

Rusted Root. 1994. "Drum Trip." On *When I Woke.* Polygram 522713.

A Tribe Called Quest. 1996. "Phony Rappers." On *Beats, Rhymes and Life.* Jive 41587.

Various artists. 2002. *Music from and Inspired by the Motion Picture 8 Mile.* Shady/Interscope Records 493508.

———. 2002. *More Music from 8 Mile.* Shady/Interscope Records 450979.

Listening to the Music of the Brooklyn-based Rapper Sensational

Evan Rapport

My goal in this chapter is to analyze a hip hop recording as a sound object by identifying and interpreting analytical and theoretical constructs held by a community of listeners. I use concepts and terms gleaned from interviews and discussions in order to make social experience and context integral parts of the analysis from the outset.[1] My own interpretations and the use of notation and transcription became a part of the process, but they are not the starting points.

I chose a recording that might resist analysis employing familiar musicological tools and the methods in which I myself have been trained to interpret music. My selection for this purpose was *Loaded with Power* by the artist Sensational, released in 1997 on the Brooklyn-based WordSound label.[2] Sensational, formerly known as Torture, was a participant in the Jungle Brothers' 1993 release, *J. Beez Wit the Remedy*—now a cult favorite but at the time a poor seller for Warner Brothers. Since *Loaded with Power*, Sensational has since released albums for WordSound almost every year, including *Corner the Market* (1999), *Heavy-weighter* (2000), and *Natural Shine* (2002), as well as an album for the record label Ipecac, *Get on My Page* (2001). Much of Sensational's music eschews typical hip hop production techniques, commercial song forms, and norms of flow. Though I always have enjoyed the music and, at times, been able to articulate reasons why, *Loaded with Power* has continuously eluded my cognitive analysis and categorization. A reception-based analysis illuminates the music in a way that an analysis proceeding primarily from my own interpretation and listening does not.[3]

My initial strategy was to canvass as wide a range of hip hop listeners as possible. I sent out email invitations, created a website where certain tracks could be previewed for uninitiated listeners, and alerted friends versed in hip hop culture to the project. I made my project known to an approximately equal number of men and women, and I also tried to include a variety of generations.[4] I also compiled comments about Sensational found on the Internet, located on sites that provide recording reviews (such as the *All-Music Guide,* allmusic.com), sales copy, or bulletin board postings (primarily the USENET group rec.music.hip-hop).[5]

Despite my attempts to include females and people of various ages, my respondents overwhelmingly were males in their twenties or early thirties. From this group, those most interested in the project and willing to grant extensive interviews were serious fans with extensive knowledge of obscure artists, many already fans of Sensational's music. The end result was, in effect, a self-selected group of respondents with shared values and interests, providing an interpretive community of young male hip hop enthusiasts.[6] I hope that what emerges from the words of this community is a suitable framework for understanding Sensational's music, which is after all the ultimate object of the analysis.

My data come from twenty-five different sources and five different genres of responses. Appendix A lists the names of the commentators by type of responses, which include sales copy, record reviews, or comments on rec.music.hip-hop, as well as commentary created directly for this project through informal discussion and interviews.[7] This study draws heavily on the interviews, which conveyed the greatest range of nuanced responses; i.e., I could hear tone of voice and inflection, laughter, and at times, watch movement. Furthermore, those who agreed to interviews also continued to discuss the subject with me and to comment on interview transcriptions.

Analytical Categories

After compiling the responses, I divided the comments into four analytical categories: (1) General style, (2) Flow, (3) Beats, and (4) Production values. I created these categories by determining which aspects of Sensational's music a commentator addressed, and then grouping the aspects that occurred most frequently. (Appendix B lists some abridged comments sorted into these categories.) Almost all of the feedback considered Sensational's music in terms of formal aesthetics and style. Frequently a commentator would move from a general description to a more specific discussion in which the sound was divided into two parts—the rapping ("flow") and the underlying music (called "beats," or sometimes just "the music")—also a convention of hip hop critical discourse (see, e.g., Walser 1995; Keyes 2002; Krims 2000; and Miyakawa 2005). A number of comments addressed the less commonly explored subject of production values (sound quality and timbres), and this warranted a separate category. Comparisons with other artists frequently helped elucidate points. Because this study is concerned with stylistic characteristics of the music as a sound object, as well as the fact that most of the responses addressed those particular aspects, I analyzed comments less directly concerned with sound—themes and topics covered in Sensational's lyrics; his attitudes, stances, and intentions; the context in which one might listen to his music[8]—in terms of the four main categories.

These analytical categories then provide the interpretive framework for the following reading of Sensational's music. Although these categories are to some extent artificial, the frequency with which some descriptions, concepts, and terms recur is an indication of the theoretical constructs that comprise the interpretive habits of many hip hop listeners.

1. General style

Perhaps the most common way in which listeners discuss Sensational's style in general terms is to emphasize his uniqueness. He is "a unique rapper all by himself out there" (IR). Many comments positioned uniqueness as a positive value in and of itself, almost parallel to the quality of "complexity" in much musicological discourse (see, e.g., the discussion on complexity in Walser 1995). Uniqueness is of a higher priority than skill *per se*: "No one else raps like this guy. I don't think anybody else would *choose* to rap like it, you know [laughter], but he does it, and he doesn't stop" (IR). Furthermore, Sensational's unique style importantly demonstrates an ability to transfer his personality directly into his music without any artificiality. Two interviewees, for example, described listening to Sensational's music as being "inside his brain" or his style as "coming straight out of his mind" (NR; IR). His style is "raw" (SF) and "pure" (SF; NR; Ha).

It is also notable that listeners believe that Sensational is an eccentric, charismatic individual. He is "fucked up" (RdA; Ci; IR; SF; NR); "pure craziness" (Ha); "out there" (Ar; Ha); "really sick" (RdA)—that is, a non-conformist. He is unable to do anything "normal" (SF), he's "in his own world" (NR), and because of his distinctive style, his music fares well when pitted against other hip hop artists and records, the majority of which are "boring" or "cookie-cutter" (NR; IR), no matter how virtuosic their technique might be. Copying someone else's style yields the dullest hip hop; there needs to be at least some sort of "flip" (IR). Sensational exploits a hyperpersonal approach to rapping and music-making, flying in the face of the mainstream styles and sounds. He himself seems to know that his uniqueness is part of his appeal. On the inside cover to *Corner the Market*, he writes in capital letters, "THANKS TO MY STYLE / NO THANKS TO FAKE MOTHERFUCKERS."

Listeners associate Sensational with other rappers and musicians who are also seen as eccentrics and non-conformists: Kool Keith (Aq; Ws), Ol' Dirty Bastard (Ws; SH), Busta Rhymes (SH); Prince Paul (Ci); Sun Ra and Lee Perry (Ws; SF). Paradoxically, what all of these individuals have in common is how unlike everyone else they are. In an article that draws connections among Sun Ra, Lee Perry, and George Clinton (of P-Funk), John Corbett cites precedents for this aesthetic: "In African-American slang there is a longstanding constellation of terms that revolves around the interrogation of sanity. Subtle and supple, this group of words relies on a set of interrelated connotations—a certain fluidity of meaning—that links madness with excellence and innovation. For example: 'crazy,' 'wild,' 'out of control,' 'nutty,' 'insane,' 'out'" (Corbett 1994: 13). Hence, when listeners use such terms to describe Sensational, they are placing him in a tradition that is oriented around uniqueness and eccentricity as core virtues.

On the one hand, these qualities are commonly evoked as being distinctive to modernist or American attitudes. Western artistic traditions have regularly lauded the eccentric genius, beholden to no one but his or her own muse and personal vision. White composers such as Carl Ruggles and Harry Partch provide parallels to the aesthetic of eccentricity Corbett associates with Black artists. Such comparisons open up a space for considering attitudes and approaches that are not divided along race lines, but rather, are part of the modern condition. Measured by the categories and qualities of uniqueness, eccentricity, personal vision, and genius, hip hop seems to be created within a modernist worldview, and not a postmodern one (characterized by "depthlessness," superficiality, the perception of the object world as simulacra, the disposition of the subject, the "waning of affect," and pastiche [Jameson 1990: 6-9, 16]). The collage-like techniques of sample-based music should not necessarily imply a postmodern outlook.

On the other hand, Sensational is often characterized as working in opposition to mainstream aesthetics, resulting in negative definitions—in other words, rather than describing what Sensational is, people describe what he *is not*. One set of negative definitions of Sensational is that he creates non-music, which can be applied directly to a perceived avoidance of hip hop's aesthetic values (non-rapping, non-beats). This characterization may be criticism (Sensational "doesn't sound like he's trying to make music" [Ci]) or praise. When a discourse of "non-music" is considered appealing or indicative of innovation, it seems appropriate to invoke the attitudes of postmodernists interested in an "anti-aesthetic" formulated around process and chance as ends in themselves, and defined in opposition to general assumptions about the nature of art (cf. Ulmer 1983: 101 on the music of John Cage). Rather than representing either modernism or postmodernism, Sensational's music provides a locus for examining the complex interactions of both modern and postmodern aesthetics and worldviews.[9]

Another negative characterization is posited by Corbett, who frames the sounds, rhetoric, and gestures of Black eccentrics as being intentionally "not of this world" (1994: 8), inverting the commonsense notion of sanity in order to illuminate the actual insanity of real life (a philosophical outlook shared by many mystical doctrines). The danger in Corbett's "Brother from Another Planet" analysis might be to conflate an artist's transcendent mythmaking tendencies with his or her musical contributions, which are actually strongly situated in specific musical traditions. Sensational, like the innovators with whom he is associated, is very much concerned with the clearly defined aesthetic norms and conventions associated with the genre in which he works. His creative manipulation of hip hop rules situates him in the tradition, not outside of it. Two respondents described his music in relation to overriding hip hop aesthetics in these remarkably similar terms: "It was about hip hop but at the same time the farthest thing from it" (SF) and "a hip hop record that isn't hip hop in any way" (NR). In other words, Sensational is in many ways clearly positioned in the hip hop universe, but part of his individuality comes from the many ways that he resists the norms.[10] It is in the context of hip hop (or perhaps, post-hip hop) that Sensational's music makes the most sense.

2. Flow

When commentators focus on more specific aspects of Sensational's music, definite characteristics begin to emerge. His lyrical style, or flow, is described as "mumbled" (Aq; RdA; BA), "off-beat" (Ws; SH), "tripped-out" (Ws), or "blunted" (Ws; TZ). He is definitely *not* generally considered a rapper with flashy, astounding skills. More often people might say he "doesn't really bother to rap" (BA) or "half the time he just mumbles to himself" (RdA); his word choices are "incredibly repetitive" (MM). To top it off, Sensational likes to obscure his words with various electronic effects.

His approach is "stream-of-consciousness" (IR; NR), a "lazy-ass dumb style that [is] like only for himself" (IR) and heard as "freestyling" (TZ; IR; NR; CH). But if he's freestyling, it is certainly a very different kind than the displays of lightning-quick rhyming captured by such groups as Freestyle Fellowship (for example, on their 1993 release *Innercity Griots*). One interviewee illustrated this point with an example from "Where it Started At" (transcribed as Figure 1): "Stream-of-consciousness isn't exactly the right word. He seems to be freestyling but then he loses interest in what he's saying and shit—you know that part on track two or three where he's saying 'gotta gotta gotta ... AIM' and you're like, 'that's the best you could think of?' But for some reason, it isn't boring" (NR). Notice that Sensational takes two full measures to riff rhythmically on "gotta" before the word "aim," which is emphasized in volume and by appearing squarely in its position on beat one of the next cycle.

Figure 1. From "Where it Started At," *Loaded with Power*. Example starts at 1:13.

1		2		3		4	
							What I
preach is		naturally me			Tele-	grams	
	I get	paid to send			Like		
			I	get paid to		entertain I	
gotta			gotta		gotta	gotta gotta	
	gotta	gotta			gotta	gotta gotta	
AIM							

Sensational's frequent collaborator Skiz Fernando informed me that usually Sensational is in fact *not* freestyling, and that he wrote most of what is heard on *Loaded with Power*.

> ER: Is it mostly freestyling?
> SF: Well, *Loaded with Power* he did all at home, so he made the beats and wrote
> to it and then recorded it. But he won't re-record shit so he'll ad lib and leave stuff

in there. He'll have an ad lib track, so there's freestyling there. If he messes up on the original track, he might cover it up with the ad lib track.
ER: Oh, that makes sense.
SF: But I'd get mad at him, 'cause he'd be over my house and he'd just freestyle. And I'd say "you gotta write! I can't listen to you say, 'Yo!' [pauses] 'Sensational!' over and over!" [loud laughter]

Sensational always keeps first takes and leaves in mistakes and accidents, resulting in a freestyling-*sounding* flow that adds to the "pure," non-artificial aesthetic, and of course, a very idiosyncratic "non-rapping" style that adds to Sensational's uniqueness. His approach to interpreting his compositions in this way is also similar to the way Sun Ra would keep first takes and loosely interpret pre-composed material on the fly.[11] Fernando also notes that live, first-take energy and incorporating mistakes is also part of the hip hop tradition, as early DJs might utilize "accidents" such as skipping records into their performances (SF).

Sensational also has a dazed-and-confused "cottony flow" (PS), connected to his penchant for marijuana (note his many song titles like "Chunky Buds" on *Corner the Market*). "I doubt if a single track on any of Sensational's albums has been recorded out from under the influence" (TM). He "rhymes like he can't remember where he is or his own name" (RdA). His words are "blunted poetry-in-motion sickness" (Ws). Listening to "Jigglin' What You Like to See,"[12] at 4'22" (shown in Figure 2), one interviewee began laughing (Sensational is often also described as "funny" [Ha; TM] and laughter is a common response), and remarked, "Well, you know … just from my experience with doing rap … if you do it really high like that, that's all that comes out. You're just like on that beat, like, 'aaaahhh'" (IR). As is evident in the timing chart, Sensational is not especially eager to show off his rhyming skills; in a six-minute song, he only rhymes for about forty-eight seconds, from 0:23 to 1:11, and even there it is a bit spotty. Instead, Sensational is rhythmically "riding" the beat, similar to the eight "gotta" beats of Figure 1, relaxed and free. Whether or not a direct correlation can be made between Sensational's flow and the physiological effects of being stoned (after all, many rappers boast about smoking marijuana with very different results), part of Sensational's unique style is attributed to his efforts to capture an atmosphere of being high. Some people have also commented that his music might be best appreciated while being stoned (CH; TM).[13]

Figure 2. From "Jigglin' What You Like to See," *Loaded with Power*.

0:00 - 0:22	freestyled introduction
0:23 - 1:11	rapping (with rhyming)
1:11 - 1:18	beat instrumental
1:18 - 1:40	variations on words "wiggle-jiggle"
1:40 - 1:45	"wiggle-jiggle" with effects
1:45 - 2:02	"wiggle-jiggle" without effects
2:02 - 3:06	freestyling (little rhyming)
3:06 - 3:20	"wiggle-jiggle" without effects
3:20 - 3:40	"wiggle-jiggle" with effects
3:40 - 4:15	"wiggle-jiggle" without effects
4:15 - 4:22	"wiggle-jiggle" with effects
4:22 - 5:19	freestyling (little rhyming)
5:19 - 6:10	"wiggle-jiggle" with effects

Finally, although much of Sensational's music is highly unconventional in hip hop, the topics he addresses are typical of the genre. He "is always rapping abuot [*sic*] I am dope, you are wack, I smoke blunts, I like to fuck bitches" (TZ), or "standard hip hop concerns" such as "boasting about his record sales," "bragging about his income," or "proclaiming himself the king of hip hop" (all VV). He covers "drug topics and bombast almost exclusively" (MD). But although these topics are common to hip hop, for some, the fact that he has such an extremely narrow range of topics and a strong single-mindedness in covering them adds to his uniqueness: he has "trademark self-aggrandizing rhymes" (RA).[14] These topics can also seem odd when compared with the reality of Sensational as an underground rapper with rather unimpressive record sales when compared with mainstream rap stars.[15] However, these topics are an important way that Sensational remains connected to the rap genre while he is on the fringes in many other respects.

3. Beats
Sensational's lyrical style and beats are linked by the fact that he generally creates both of these aspects of the music himself—especially the case on *Loaded with Power*. As with the claim that he "doesn't really bother to rap" (BA), many of Sensational's beats demonstrate a similar sort of anti-aesthetic: one beat ("Skit n' Skatterin'") was described as "it almost could be a beat but it doesn't quite make it" (NR). And like everything else about Sensational, the beats can be described as "fucked-up" and "distorted" (SF; NR). The unorthodoxy of Sensational's beats at times needs to be explained in terms of other genres besides hip hop: one person called the beat on "Freak Styler" "a hip hop version of drum 'n' bass" (DA), another called "Skit n' Skatterin'" "industrial" (NR). Together, the combination of Sensational's rapping and beat style might be described as "some insane type guy

mumbling to himself over some noise he creates" (Ha).

One of the key elements of Sensational's peculiar beats is that he plays all the parts himself, and even if he samples something he will "play it live on the keyboard, and that's how he gets a lot of ill shit" (SF). Sensational will keep "mistakes" and patterns that are looped incorrectly (SF), a clear parallel to his loose, freestyle-sounding approach to flow. (As shown in Figure 3, a handwritten message complete with cross-out on the *Corner the Market*'s CD face, this aesthetic carries over into his visual style.) Fernando explained that Sensational insisted on keeping the earliest attempts to loop a beat, without going through the usual process of aligning the loop to a regular pulse. The loops are also very short, usually four beats long, related to the limitations of Sensational's sampler—a four-track mixer (SF). Sensational exploits the fundamental nature of a "loop" by turning anything, no matter how chaotic or uncontrolled, into a pattern simply by repeating it or triggering it manually at regular intervals. Perhaps unsurprisingly, Sensational might subvert the "loop" while simultaneously emphasizing its essence as a loop. On "I Like Crispies" (*Loaded with Power*), for example, the rhythm of a warbly vocal melody barely lines up with the underlying metrical grid, and although the pattern usually enters on the first pulse of the meter, frequently and inconsistently it is early or late. The result is "controlled chaos" (SF), and the unpredictability is something almost fundamentally opposed to the almost obsessive level of control associated with the producer described in Schloss's (2004) or Miyakawa's (2005) writings.

Figure 3. *Corner the Market,* detail of CD face corner.

Sensational's beats can also be "minimal" (MM), "exquisitely junky synth minimalism" (PS), or "static loop[s]" (Ha). The beat for "When I Deal Minze" (Example 1), for example, is constructed almost completely of two elements—a low synthesized sound and a distorted backbeat[16]—and hardly changes throughout the entire song. And rather than fitting his loops into rigid song forms, Sensational leaves the "thick and irregular" (MM) "broken beats" (Ws) repetitive and open-ended, providing a foundation for his stream-of-consciousness delivery. Formal divisions such as choruses are largely distinguished by verbal repetitions rather than a change of melody or beat texture (in "When I Deal Minze," the only indication of the chorus is the change in the lyrics, four times through the line "hit

Example 1. From "When I Deal Minze," *Loaded with Power.*

Chorus:

Chorus (with beat turned around):

Freestyling:
[With echo] Yo yo this isn't an imitation, this is Sensational, aka Perfection
[...] beats flowin', you know what I'm sayin'?
This is how I do it ... original, know what I'm sayin'?
I ain't tryin' to sound like nobody over here, Yo yo

Chorus:
Hit after hit, make ya head spin (4x) [see above]

Verse:
If you really want it
You can get it
Anything in life
My criminal outfit
Color album speak on it
Smackin' dealers up
Who try to front on the hand
I be the one from the Crown Heights area
King size everything
Shout out to the MC rhythm
Refreshin' their memory
Freak Sensational
Got strategy

Chorus:
Hit after hit, make ya head spin (4x)

after hit, make ya head spin"). Rather than being an anomaly, however, this mini-malist type of beat is part of a venerable hip hop tradition, the very essence of this aesthetic actually being the breakbeat itself.[17]

Fernando compares Sensational's approach in the studio to that of dub musi-cian/producer Lee Perry. Both have a definite vision that they are trying to articu-late, exploring a number of aesthetic directions by using the studio as a compositional tool. Like Perry, Sensational takes fragments of melodies and man-ually "plays" them in unpredictable ways. They both also revel in effects such as echo, reverb, and distortion, used to obfuscate or emphasize lyrics and various timbres. Finally, as with the dub aesthetic more generally, Sensational explores the repetitive nature of beats and loops in and of themselves rather than using them in the service of standard pop-song forms. As David Toop notes, "Lee Perry explored the potential of sound to hypnotize" (1995: 114) and that dub "spread[s] out a song or a groove over a vast landscape of peaks and deep trenches, extending hooks and beats to vanishing point ..." (115).

4. Production values

Never one to conform to expected standards, Sensational's production values are notoriously "lo-fi" or "no-fi" (Ws; Ha; Wh), "mushy" (DA), and yes, "distorted" (AL; CH) and "fucked-up" (SF; NR). The production sounds "like a Casio key-board in a cardboard box being hit with a hammer" (RdA) or "like someone's fry-ing chicken in the background" (SF). In fact, his music was used as a point of comparison for another's music: "[an album by Mos Def] reminded me of Sensational the sound was so bad" (Ar). As with his rap style and beats, his "dirty" (SF) production can either be an appealing aspect of Sensational's music for peo-ple or a serious detraction. Fernando commented, for example, on the lack of interest for Sensational in "the hood," which he partially chalks up to the sound of current popular "squeaky-clean" productions.[18] Indeed, much of the plot of *Crooked,* a film made by Fernando starring Sensational and based loosely on his life, relies on an A&R man's demand that Sensational clean up his music in order to make it market-ready.

The low production values may be largely a result of Sensational's equipment and lack of access to expensive studios rather than an aesthetic preference. The lyrics on *Loaded with Power,* for example, were all recorded using a pair of head-phones as a microphone, as Sensational did not own a mic at the time (SF). However, on various occasions Sensational uses low-fidelity timbres as the basis of the track, creating dense and thick textures such as the one heard on "Skit n' Skatterin'" (Track 4 on *Loaded with Power*). This is one of Sensational's versions of complexity: not tightly gridded patterns but layered loops that become almost indistinguishable from one another. This can be clearly identified as an intentional aesthetic move. Even though the production values are increased on subsequent albums, the basic approach to beat-making and the resulting sound is remarkably consistent throughout all of his albums.

Conclusion

In this study, I have endeavored to outline Sensational's style by starting with the words of listeners, fans, and participants in hip hop culture and music-making. The listeners represented here engage with hip hop music in accordance with a strong sense of aesthetics and theory, amounting to a style of interpretation. Interpretation, the way in which one hears and thinks about music, is heavily based on knowledge regarding formal musical characteristics, such as general style, flow, beats, and production techniques (resulting in different timbral qualities). Ideas and assumptions about these musical properties are part of larger analytical categories that are identifiable by descriptive terms and phrases as well as comparisons with other artists and negative definitions.

What I hope has emerged in this analysis is not only a portrait of a consummately individual artist with an innovative approach to hip hop music-making, but also a glimpse of a community of listeners and practitioners who share an aesthetic of uniqueness, innovation, and boundary-stretching, and who are also discussing their interests and ideas in new forums like USENET. There are many artists like Sensational, not only in hip hop but other genres such as rock, dub, trance, and ambient (Toop 1995), who are creating music oriented around minimal production, pot-addled sensibilities, and the exploration of "mistakes." Much of this type of music is ignored by those analyzing music in the academy because of the mismatch of the music's aesthetic goals with standard analytical methods that were created in tandem with other musical practices, or the values cultivated by such practices. After all, music scholars, like the hip hop listeners and practitioners whom I have considered in this paper, apply analytical constructs that they have learned and practiced through socialization in a particular interpretive community. These analytical techniques have historically thrived on elucidating complexities or hidden structures and meanings in music, and specifically, the corpus generally referred to as the Western canon. Music outside of the Western canon, such as hip hop, can be difficult to approach with the same tools, especially when the music does not seem to have the features generally demonstrated by objects of musicological study. Those wishing to analyze non-canonical styles of music must either legitimize the music to the academic community by demonstrating that these features do exist in the music under discussion[19] and by referencing published scholarly work to buttress the argument, or else take a different approach altogether. Affirming such music on familiar terms might have the important effect of including neglected figures in the Western canon. But music that is both non-canonical and resistant to musicological analysis necessitates the use of different methods. If we take seriously responses by listeners, creative theoretical frameworks and interpretative strategies can emerge, pointing the way to engage the music on its own terms.

APPENDIX A. Responses and commentators.

Abbreviations:

AL:	A. Lu
Aq:	Aquarius Records website
Ar:	"Aristotle"
BA:	Ben Axelrad
CH:	Clayton Harper
Ci:	"Citywide13"
DA:	D. Arbit
Ha:	"HaSSaSSiN"
IR:	Isaac Ramos
MD:	M. F. DiBella
MM:	Michaelangelo Matos
Na:	"Natty GoGo"
NR:	Nat Rabb
PS:	Peter S. Scholtes
RA:	Rick Anderson
RdA:	Richard D. Allen
SF:	Skiz Fernando
SH:	Steve Huey
Sq:	"Squirrel Police"
TM:	Taylor McLaren
TS:	Tim Schnetgoeke
TZ:	"TZArecta"
VV:	Victor W. Valdivia
Wh:	"Whatdaumm"
Ws:	WordSound website

Phone Interviews
- Skiz Fernando (aka Spectre, SKZA): owner of WordSound records and producer on many Sensational tracks and recordings. Interview conducted 25 April 2004.
- Nat Rabb (aka San Serac): Introduced me to Sensational's music in 1997, was a member of Baltimore's Narcoleptics and currently produces his own brand of dance music. Interview conducted 25 April 2004.

In-Person Interviews
- Isaac Ramos: Runs Dogg and Pony Records, was and is part of various bands (Dogg and Pony, Castro). Interview conducted 20 April 2004.

Email comments and informal discussions concerning two tracks available for previewing on a website set up by me. The songs are "Freak Styler" and "Jigglin' What You Like to See," from *Loaded with Power*, but there is no indication as to the artist or the song titles.
- Clayton Harper: friend (male). He recognized the music as Sensational's. Email sent 23 April 2004.
- A. Lu: student at Hunter College (male). Email sent 4 May 2004.
- D. Arbit: student at Hunter College (female).

Sales Copy (from Internet)
- WordSound website (much of which was probably written or influenced by Skiz Fernando, see "interviews," above).
- Aquarius records (Byram). http://www.aquariusrecords.org/cat/byram8.html.

Record Reviews
- Michaelangelo Matos. Review of *Heavyweighter* (Matos 2000).
- Peter S. Scholtes. Review of *Get on My Page* (Scholtes 2001).
- Steve Huey. Review of *Loaded with Power* and *Corner the Market* (Huey n.d.).
- Rick Anderson. Review of *Natural Shine* (Anderson n.d.).
- Victor W. Valdivia. Review of *Heavyweighter* (Valdivia n.d.).
- M.F. DiBella. Review of *Get on My Page* (DiBella n.d.).

USENET (rec.music.hip-hop)
- HaSSaSSiN. Posting 10 November 1998 in thread "Torture?" and 21 April 1998 in thread "What's the last CD you bought and how was it?".
- Richard D. Allen. Posting 11 November 1998 in thread "Torture?" and 14 April 1998 in thread "Flash whas the deal on this artist sensational."
- Aristotle. Posting 11 September 1999 in thread "Song of the year so far......" and 13 September 1999 in thread "How is the new 'sensational' lp??".
- Natty GoGo. Posting 12 August 2001 in thread "Wordsound."
- Squirrel Police. Posting 9 February 2003 in thread "Recommend me some hip hop."
- Tim Schnetgoeke. Posting 4 March 2003 in thread "Live shows."
- Taylor McLaren. Posting 24 July 2001 in thread "Songs to smoke bud to."
- TZArecta. Posting 22 September 1999 in thread "Sensational-Corner the market."
- Whatdaumm. Posting 13-14 September 1999 in thread "How is the new 'sensational' lp??".
- Citywide13. Posting 15 April 1998 in thread "Flash whas the deal on this artist sensational."
- Ben Axelrad. Posting 15 April 1998 in thread "Flash whas the deal on this artist sensational."

APPENDIX B. Analytical categories with comments (abridged). Comments by different respondents are separated by semicolons and grouped together by common use of terminology or by expression of similar ideas.

1. General style
- one of the most fucked-up rappers we know; literally fucked up; crazily fucked up; one of the most fucked-up hip hop records I've ever heard
- purest form of making music that there is; totally pure; purest essence
- Its pretty OUT THERE; out there; Pure craziness
- really sick and because of that I really liked it for a while
- I doubt if a single track on any of Sensational's albums has been recorded out from under the influence; This song is pretty pot-ad[d]led; I think the artist is trying to communicate the effects of how much pot he has smoked; like the old blunted bastard
- coming from somewhere I don't know where it's coming from, you know, just sound like it comes straight outta this guy's mind; in his own world; inside his brain
- unique rapper all by himself out there; unique style
- it was hip hop but at the same time the furthest thing from it; a hip hop record that isn't hip hop in any way
- completely unorthodox; he couldn't do anything normal
- doesn't sound like he's trying to make music
- [Comparisons to styles of other hip hop artists]: Wu-Tang with a head injury; more favorite than Kool Keith; a breed apart from these koo-koo MCs (Kool Keith, Old Dirty Bastard); reminiscent of Ol' Dirty Bastard or Busta Rhymes; its hip hop? I dunno what it is; more insane than [T]ricky; more fucked up than [Prince Paul's] *Psychoanalysis*; closest I think to Divine Styler

2. Flow (lyrical style)
- he's funny as hell
- mumbled with a mouthful of marbles; insane type guy mumbling to himself over some noise he creates; half the time he just mumbles to himself; start a rhyme and just stop, talk, mumble, whatever
- blunted poetry-in-motion-sickness; cottony flow
- lazy-ass dumb style that was like only for himself, I love that about him; rhymes like he can't remember where he is or his own name; sounds like he's just freestyling the whole time; you can just tell he's freestyling most of it; doesn't really bother to rap; doesn't even rap; stream-of-conscious [*sic*]; stream-of-consciousness
- utterly mental words of wisdom; his voice and the cadences of his speech fascinate me; actually has a distinct flow; [high] level of abstraction; intimate; weird; unfettered; turning on the faucet of his brain; no inhibitions; bizarre charisma

3. Beats ("the music")
- minimal; static loop; fucked-up beats; fucked-up; it's all distorted
- almost could be a beat but it doesn't quite make it; broken beats; thick and irregular; deeply off-kilter; not even really a beat; dusted; weird stumbling quality; dream-like quality; bizarre; very experiemental [*sic*]
- doesn't sound like he's sampling at all either; really incoherent noises and shit over really annoying beats; beats that sounded like flipping the channels on a TV

4. Production values (sound quality, timbres)

- no-fi music; crazy low fi dissonant shit; lo-fi ambience; no-fi production [re: *Corner the Market*]; l like him because just of his style and production lo fi
- exquisitely junky synth minimalism; production sounds like a Casio keyboard in a cardboard box being hit with a hammer; like someone's frying chicken in the background
- vocals were all distorted; everything was all distorted and fucked up; distorted bass drum
- [Sensational's music is unlike] hip hop today[, which] is slick, clean, squeaky-clean; how much more fucked up it is than anything else [in hip hop]
- whippin sound; noise; basement super basement shit; dusted productions; kitchen-cupboard percussion; overmodulated drum track; tinty snare sound

Acknowledgments

I would especially like to thank Ellie Hisama for the time and energy she dedicated to editing my own paper as well as to this entire publication and the seminar. I would also like to thank Skiz Fernando, Nat Rabb, Isaac Ramos, Eric Hatch, all of the other respondents, and of course, Sensational. I am indebted to feedback and support from Dave Pier, Stephen Blum, Sarah Vezina, Jerry Lim, and my fellow students in the seminar.

Lyrics, transcriptions, and images are printed with permission of WordSound Recordings.

Notes

1. Other analyses of hip hop taking a similar approach can be found in Katz (2004) and Schloss (2004), although these authors focus on practitioners discussing their own creative activities.

2. WordSound is owned and operated by Skiz Fernando, who is also the executive producer and engineer of many of Sensational's records. Currently he runs the label from Baltimore, Maryland. More information about WordSound can be found at www.wordsound.com.

3. Although I am focusing on *Loaded with Power,* Sensational's other recordings conform to similar aesthetic principles and are naturally referenced by a number of people in this study.

4. For example, I made numerous announcements and pleas for participation to students enrolled in the World Music survey course that I taught at Hunter College (Spring 2004). The class was composed of 53 females and 13 males covering a wide range of ages and many different ethnic backgrounds.

5. USENET is a bulletin-board-type internet forum in which participants "post" articles in "threads" revolving around specific topics.

6. Many posting to USENET use aliases, and gender can be masked, making it risky to generalize about this sample; however, all of the "real names" I encountered seemed to be male. Ethnicity was more diverse than that of age and gender, with people of white, African American, East Asian, Latino/a, and Jewish descent represented. Further complicating the homogenous picture that comes across in my study is that, according to Skiz Fernando,

Sensational has a "cult following" in Europe and Japan, and that he has a lot of female fans in those places.

7. I loosely follow Paul Berliner's method (1994: 760-62 and passim) and use a two- or three-letter abbreviation to indicate the speaker or writer. Only "published" materials, such as reviews appearing in online versions of print publications, are cited in the bibliography; USENET postings and personal communications are not.

8. Unsolicited comments about listening context were limited to getting stoned, a state that I address in my discussion of Category 2 (Flow).

9. See, e.g., the discussion of hip hop aesthetics in Manuel (1995).

10. Other features of hip hop, such as clothing and argot, are also very important for situating an artist such as Sensational in the "hip hop universe." However, a full treatment of these elements is outside the scope of this paper.

11. Just as Sensational's composed raps are often heard as freestyles, many of Sun Ra's compositions commonly identified as completely free improvisations (e.g., in Jost 1974), were, based on copyrighted scores in the Library of Congress, probably heavily pre-composed but performed with a style that allowed for a great amount of interpretive freedom.

12. This track, Track 18, was produced by Skiz Fernando and is the only one on *Loaded with Power* not produced by Sensational. It is misnumbered on the CD case as Track 17.

13. Incidentally, pot smoking was the only area in which Sensational's music was discussed by listeners in terms of uses and practices as opposed to formal aesthetics.

14. That lyrical topics were greatly discussed by record reviewers, but almost nobody else, may suggest that this may be an area in which occupational demands result in different listening habits and expectations among the different commentators.

15. Fernando was unsure of the exact figures, but noted that he did not think that *Loaded with Power* sold over 1,000 copies.

16. Although I refer to a backbeat, the rhythm is "turned around" throughout the song. Example 1 shows the refrain in both positions.

17. The breakbeat evolved because the favorite sections for many dancers were the moments in which all of the complexities of layered patterns and song-form divisions were stripped away; DJs then extended these sections, which also became the preferred underlying texture for MCs to rap over. Fricke and Ahearn write, "The percussion breaks—where most of the band drops out, leaving the drummer and percussionists to carry the music— were the parts that the b-boys liked, and the hip-hop forefathers developed a way to extend those breaks, alternating between the same section of the song on two records on different turntables" (2002:23). Many classic beats, even those composed with drum machines and keyboards in studios with multi-tracking capabilities, seem to aspire to a "minimalist" breakbeat aesthetic—in order to create the most sophisticated, creative, and interesting beat possible that remains sparse enough to leave room for the MC and, most importantly, provokes movement such as dancing or head-nodding (examples might include Run DMC's "It's Like That," Audio Two's "Top Billing," or Boogie Down Productions' "The Bridge is Over"). After all, the human beatbox, exemplified by Doug E. Fresh's beats for Slick Rick, is only physically able to layer two simultaneous timbres, one created by the lips or tongue and the other by vibration of the vocal chords.

18. Another non-conformist musician who also released many independent records with lo-fi production is Sun Ra, who, as mentioned previously, is a point of comparison for Sensational. And like Sensational, Sun Ra at times had difficulty getting a positive response from the "hood." In an interview with Art Taylor, Betty Carter said, "[Sun Ra is] nothing

but bullshit. Sun Ra has got whitey going for it. He couldn't go uptown and do that to blackie. He would be chased off the stage in Harlem or in Bedford-Stuyvesant" (Taylor [1977] 1993: 279).

19. For example, Robert Walser explains his use of transcription in his article on Public Enemy's "Fight the Power" as "a way of opening up for discussion the musical details of a style that many people do not *think* has musical details" (1995: 200, emphasis in original), demonstrating "coherence and complexity ... precisely what have been denied to hip hop ..." (199-200).

References

Anderson, Rick. n.d. Review of *Natural Shine*, by Sensational. *All Music Guide*, http://www.allmusic.com (accessed 20 April 2004).

Berliner, Paul. 1994. *Thinking in Jazz*. Chicago: University of Chicago Press.

Corbett, John. 1994. *Extended Play: Sounding Off from John Cage to Dr. Funkenstein*. Durham: Duke University Press.

DiBella, M. F. n.d. Review of *Get on My Page*, by Sensational. *All Music Guide*, http://www.allmusic.com (accessed 20 April 2004).

Fricke, Jim, and Charlie Ahearn. 2002. *Yes Yes Y'all: The Experience Music Project Oral History of Hip-Hop's First Decade*. Oxford: Perseus Press.

Huey, Steve. n.d. Review of *Loaded with Power*, by Sensational. *All Music Guide*, http://www.allmusic.com (accessed 20 April 2004).

———. n.d. Review of *Corner the Market*, by Sensational. *All Music Guide*, http://www.all-music.com (accessed 20 April 2004).

Jameson, Frederic. 1995. *Postmodernism, or the Logic of Late Capitalism*. Durham: Duke University Press.

Jost, Ekkehard. 1974. *Free Jazz*. New York: Da Capo Press.

Katz, Mark. 2004. "The Turntable as Weapon: Understanding the DJ Battle." Chap. 6 in *Capturing Sound: How Technology has Changed Music*. Berkeley: University of California Press.

Keyes, Cheryl. 2002. *Rap Music and Street Consciousness*. Urbana: University of Illinois Press.

Krims, Adam. 2000. *Rap Music and the Poetics of Identity*. Cambridge: Cambridge University Press.

Manuel, Peter. 1995. "Music as Symbol, Music as Simulacrum: Postmodern, Pre-modern, and Modern Aesthetics in Subcultural Popular Musics." *Popular Music* 14(2): 227-39.

Matos, Michaelangelo. 2000. Review of *Heavyweighter*, by Sensational. *Seattle Weekly*, 19-25 October. http://www.seattleweekly.com/features/0042/cd-staff.shtml (accessed 20 April 2004).

Miyakawa, Felicia. 2005. *Five Percenter Rap: God Hop's Music, Message, and Black Muslim Mission*. Bloomington: Indiana University Press.

Schloss, Joseph G. 2004. *Making Beats: The Art of Sample-Based Hip-Hop*. Hanover, NH: Wesleyan University Press.

Scholtes, Peter S. 2001. Review of *Get on My Page*, by Sensational. *City Pages*, 14 August. http://www.citypages.com/databank/22/1080/article9760.asp (accessed 20 April 2004).

Taylor, Arthur. [1977] 1993. *Notes and Tones: Musician-to-Musician Interviews*. New York: Da Capo Press.

Toop, David. 1995. *Ocean of Sound: Aether Talk, Ambient Sound and Imaginary Worlds*. London: Serpent's Tail.

Ulmer, Gregory. 1983. "The Object of Post-Criticism." In *The Anti-Aesthetic: Essays on Postmodern Culture*, edited by Hal Foster, 83-110. Seattle: Bay Press.

Valdivia, Victor W. n.d. Review of *Heavyweighter*, by Sensational. *All Music Guide*, http://www.allmusic.com (accessed 20 April 2004).

Walser, Robert. 1995. "Rhythm, Rhyme, and Rhetoric in the Music of Public Enemy." *Ethnomusicology* 39(2): 193-217.

Wordsound website. n.d. "Sensational: Bio," "Wordsound Catalog," and "Operation: WordSoundVision/Code Word: Crooked." http://www.wordsound.com (accessed 20 April 2004).

Discography/Filmography

Audio Two. 1988. "Top Billin.'" First Priority Music 90907.

Boogie Down Productions. 1987. "The Bridge is Over." On *Criminal Minded*. Sugar Hill 5255.

Freestyle Fellowship. 1993. *Innercity Griots*. 4th and Broadway 444050.

Fresh, Doug E., and the Get Fresh Crew. 1986. *Oh My God!* Reality F-9649.

Jungle Brothers. 1993. *J. Beez Wit the Remedy*. Warner Brothers 26679.

Run DMC. 1983. "It's Like That." Profile 1202.

Sensational. 1997. *Loaded with Power*. WordSound WSCD022.

———. 1999. *Corner the Market*. WordSound WSCD032.

———. 2000. *Heavyweighter*. WordSound WSCD037.

———. 2001. *Get on My Page*. Ipecac IPC-016.

———. 2002. *Natural Shine*. WordSound WSCD044.

Various artists. 2002. *Crooked: The Movie/The Soundtrack*. WordSound WSCD041. CD/DVD.

Wallowing in Rupture
Cultural Hybridity, Alienation, and Andre Benjamin's "A Life in the Day of Benjamin André (Incomplete)"

ROBERT WOOD

> *We cannot speak for very long, with any exactness, about "one experi-ence, one identity," without acknowledging its other side—the ruptures and discontinuities which constitute, precisely, [a culture's] "uniqueness." Cultural identity, in this sense, is a matter of "becoming" as well as of "being."*
> —Stuart Hall, "Cultural Identity and Diapora"

Hip hop, in its early twenty-first century forms, has proven resistant to easy circumscription. It is all at once popular and subversive, postmodern yet his-torically situated and is as likely to be heard as a sonic weapon, blasting from vehi-cles contending for urban spaces, as it is a vehicle for the vicarious fulfillment of fantasy by white suburban youth. It has instigated peace as often as it has violence and has contributed to the production of difference within a community not always certain as to the precise political value of such an act. These seemingly par-adoxical outgrowths atop hip hop's cultural surface have, until recently, obfuscated the values so important to hip hop's very core. But as Tricia Rose has written, scholars are beginning to understand that "rap's contradictory articulations are not signs of absent intellectual clarity; they are a common feature of community and popular cultural dialogues that always offer more than one cultural, social, or political viewpoint" (Rose 1994: 2).

Identifying the "viewpoints" or sites at which hip hop's social texts are read and then rewritten by disparate groups is invaluable for understanding the ways the genre is appropriated by and gives meaning to specific subcultures. On the super-cultural level, studies of globalization (e.g., Lipsitz 1994) have revealed the ways hip hop artists and consumers can potentially figure into subversive networks of cultural exchange through which the genre's fragmented and marginalized com-munities can unite to subvert hegemonic ideologies. Yet at the level of the individ-ual actor in cultural stagings of hip hop music, these global constructs have done little to account for the "contradictory articulations" that might be present *within individual artists*, within the idiosyncratic situations of rap musicians and their own private motivations, fantasies, and desires. As Mark Slobin notes: "There are times when we should invoke the power of hegemony, but other times when the superculture seems to be just another strand in the web of group affiliations, chosen out of aesthetic affinity" (Slobin 1993: 57). While much of hip hop *is*, in fact, undoubtedly a direct response to subaltern realities, left out of the picture are individual producers of hip hop whose music is as much inspired by the proximity of their own idiosyncratic and local cultural connections as it is by any conscious alignment with the politics of the most prominent political movements.

What interests me are the private mappings of individuals within conceptual spaces delineated by the creative traversals of singular artists whose private motivations often contradict and are alienated from explanations superimposed on them by global constructions of meaning. Using André Benjamin (André 3000)'s "A Life in the Day of Benjamin André (Incomplete)" from his 2003 CD *The Love Below* as a model, I am interested in exploring how this social alienation becomes embedded in the musical layers themselves and how these conflicting musical processes can serve as evidence of a healthy cultural hybridity, one that is omnipresent within culture at large.

> **Rolling Stone:** What else do you have planned [for your career]?
> **Andre 3000:** I want to go to Juilliard to study classical music.
> **RS:** Really? When?
> **Andre 3000:** I've been thinking about it for about a year. But things got kinda busy. This record took off. I can't be in school right now. But I'm taking saxophone and clarinet lessons. I'd study classical composition and music theory.
> (Benelli 2004)

COMING FROM ONE OF HIP HOP'S MOST POPULAR and critically acclaimed mainstream artists, Andre Benjamin's words could hardly be farther from the aspirations most frequently articulated in hip hop. In its dominant constructions, hip hop prides itself on its very distinction from these paradigms of Western culture. Through its appropriation of the turntable, for example, hip hop culture has shunned the technological determinism inherent in the common Western notion of records as finished musical products, and has proceeded to deconstruct and reassemble the content of these records into its own idiosyncratic cultural product (Katz 2004: 132). In the process, technology becomes a metaphor for an authoritarian order through which marginalized artists can potentially rise, disguised behind the mask of their abjection, to reappropriate the controlling mechanisms for their own use.

Regarding this reappropriating or "signifyin(g)" practice as found in black language, Henry Louis Gates, Jr. writes:

> By supplanting the received term's associated concept, the black vernacular tradition created a homonymic pun of the profoundest sort, thereby marking its sense

of difference from the rest of the English community of speakers. Their complex act of language Signifies upon both formal language use and its conventions, conventions established, at least officially, by middle-class white people. (Gates 1988: 46-47)

Signifyin(g), Gates continues, is "everything that must be excluded for meaning to remain coherent and linear"; it is "the Other of discourse" (Gates 1988: 50). As particular curators of such white linguistic conventions, the Juilliard School and classical music might be regarded as similar entities through which the Others of discourse might enact their subversive reappropriations. Yet Benjamin's intentions seem to lie on less overtly confrontational grounds. He has stated that he would simply "like to make more abstract music, like his hero, John Coltrane" (Tyrangiel 2003: 71). That a conservatory with a predominantly white and Asian student body might be capable of fulfilling the cultural aspirations of a black rap artist speaks of a trend towards cultural hybridity, and serves as a reminder that through globalization's increased circulation of cultural goods and means of exchange, it becomes as easy and as likely for individuals to make connections *outside* of the groups with which they are most often politically associated as it is for individuals to remain attached to these groups. "Rather than marking off boundaries and defining separate spheres of cultural practice," Juan Flores writes, "perhaps popular culture is about the transversing and transgressing of them, and characterized by a dialogic among classes and social sectors, such as the popular and non-popular, high and low, restricted and mass" (Flores quoted in Maira 2002: 37).

Andre Benjamin's desire to transverse and transgress hip hop's cultural boundaries is also manifested in his treatment of themes. Big Boi (the other half of the duo OutKast) muses:

> Battle raps go back to the early pre-dawn of hip hop and are still going on, whatever. But there's been an overabundance of "Look at my watch! Look at my car! Look at my diamonds! Look at my teeth! Look at the goddammed TV! Look it! Look it! Look it!" ... If you're doing that, what's your focus? What are you doing? Are you doing advertising for car upgrades? One big automobile commercial for the whole world? (Bozza 2000: 23)

Benjamin himself has said, "I'm not out of high school carrying guns in Cadillacs. I've got to find new things to be excited about" (Ogunnaike 2003: 87). While the search for new and novel themes by artists within popular culture is certainly not uncommon, Benjamin speaks of it with special urgency—with the desire for originality of a true modernist. His desire for new sounds—potentially even sounds from the Western classical tradition—combined with his rejection of the common hip hop tropes of violence and materialism, paint a picture of an artist alienated from the very genre in which he operates. Hip hop, for Benjamin, seems to be hardly more than a holding place, a point of maneuver from which his private pursuit of "new sounds" can find public voice.

In a manner suggesting parallels with Henri Lefebvre's conceptual spaces, Michel de Certeau writes: "[the symbolic exhibits] the voracious property that the geographical system has of being able to transform action into legibility, but in doing so it causes a way of being in the world to be forgotten" (de Certeau 1984: 97). As a figure constantly inscribing himself at the margins of official representation, somewhere in the unaccountable regions between its sanctioned categories, we might say that Benjamin's creative actions are, to a certain extent, illegible. Such an elusiveness is a direct result of Benjamin's "symbolic mobility" (Cixous and Clément 1988: 7) as an identity *becoming*, as a person whose restlessness with reified forms rebels against essentialized notions of being. As Paul Gilroy writes:

> Diaspora accentuates *becoming* rather than *being* and identity conceived diasporically, along these lines, resists reification. Foregrounding the tension around origins and essences that Diaspora brings into focus allows us to perceive that identity should not be fossilised or venerated in keeping with the holy spirit of ethnic absolutism. Identity too becomes a noun of process and it is placed on a ceaseless trial. Its almost infinite openness provides a timely alternative to the authoritarian implication of mechanical—clockwork—solidarity based on outmoded notions of "race." (Gilroy 1995: 24)

These "outmoded notions of 'race'" share with the concept of genre a certain essentialist economy that Benjamin, through his embrace of difference, clearly refutes. "A Life in the Day of Benjamin André (Incomplete)" is, instead, the embodiment of diasporic becoming, not an utterance comfortably circumscribed within one cultural type or another, and it is to this phenomenon that we now turn.

As is evident in the title, the rap tells an autobiographical story, a sort of narrative "becoming" which begins in high school and casually recalls the events up until the present day.[1] Tricia Rose reminds us of the importance of place within hip hop culture, that artists will often insist that their videos be shot on specific corners of specific neighborhoods (Rose 1994: 91); Benjamin's rap is no less than a verbal painting of these same images. As he recounts the sometimes banal minutiae of his struggle to find love and happiness, the rap proceeds to a sort of inconclusive conclusion. Before the groove fades, Benjamin remarks, "... and that's as far as I got." With this ending, "A Life in the Day" captures Benjamin's own life as an unfinished project, blurring the lines between art and life. The song's own open-ended narrative is a metaphor for identity's becoming, for the rebellion against ideological hardening.

Heightening this constantly renewed identity is the nature of the rapping itself. For the entire four-and-a-half minutes of "A Life in the Day," Benjamin raps non-stop in a manner that recalls the fluid spontaneity and stream-of-consciousness delivery of open-form freestyle. As an artist confined to the perpetual present, the freestyle improviser's dynamic relationship with his or her audience is one that insists upon the consistent deferral of expectation's fulfillment. Attempts at securing meaning are similarly deferred as the rapper and audience revel in an organic dialectical process of spontaneous creation—not in the *product* of predetermined cultural forms. As a recorded track of music, "A Life in the Day of Benjamin André (Incomplete)" manages to effectively create the "illusion of spontaneity" (Gilroy 1995: 25). Irregular rhyming contributes to the off-the-cuff effect—the listener's sensation of being-in-the-moment and of participating in a live event is further heightened by the sound of hand claps and knee slaps, providing the effect of a virtual audience directly participating in the music-making process.

Yet despite all of its simulated spontaneity and improvisational uncertainty, "A Life in the Day of Benjamin André (Incomplete)" cannot seem to overcome the normalizing effects of confinement that result when its three-dimensional effect of live performance is squeezed into the two-dimensional, bookended form on the recording. The result is a sense of alienation, palpable between the process-based spirit of Benjamin's open-ended narrative and the product-based reality demanded of it in closed, commercial form. Even the rap's concluding words, "and that's as *far* as I got" (my emphasis), which are so very different from "that's *all* I got" or simply "that's it," paradoxically imply a sense of organic unfolding while simultaneously implying the process of writing as a means of completion—a means of *being* on paper as immutable history. Speaking of this intersection between commercial culture and hip hop, Greg Dimitriadis writes: "These configurations have separated hip hop's vocal discourse (i.e., 'rap') from its early contexts of communal production, encouraging closed narrative forms over flexible word play and promoting individualised listening over community dance" (Dimitriadis 1996: 179). As the individual withdraws from the "community dance" and the improvised yields to the illusion of improvisation, the dialectical relations of give-and-take inherent in processes of becoming—in the experiential spaces connecting musician and audience—are drained, leaving nothing behind but a kind of mummified spontaneity, suspended in time. Benjamin's incomplete narrative becomes, through its reified form on record, complete in its incompletion.

As a HERMENEUTIC TOOL for understanding some of the more common features of hip hop music, Tricia Rose, after Arthur Jafa, proposes a tripartite model based on flow, layering, and rupture:

Interpreting these concepts theoretically, one can argue that they create and sustain rhythmic motion, continuity, and circularity via flow; accumulate, reinforce, and embellish this continuity through layering; and manage threats to these narratives by building in ruptures that highlight the continuity as it momentarily challenges it. These effects at the level of style and aesthetics suggest affirmative ways in which profound social dislocation and rupture can be managed and perhaps contested in the cultural arena. Let us imagine these hip hop principles as a blueprint for social resistance and affirmation: create sustaining narratives, accumulate them, layer, embellish, and transform them. However, be also prepared for rupture, find pleasure in it, in fact, *plan on* social rupture. (Rose 1994: 39, emphasis in original)

One implication of Rose's useful model is appropriately dialectical: that it is only through rupture that continuity—and ultimately, history—can be achieved. Narrative is, in many ways, an embodiment of continuity, and one of the most important features of historical narratives is their transparency to the people living within them. Much in the way that machines go unnoticed until they cease to function, narrativity is often taken for granted until attention is drawn to its binding threads. It is only after the occurrence of such "ruptures" that the importance of the personal stories individuals weave for themselves—both the linear processions of causes and effects as well as more spatial "cognitive mappings"— becomes apparent. Put another way, rupture draws attention to and therefore allows sustaining narratives by functioning negatively—by showing exactly what they are *not*.

Yet what if we consider the presence of rupture not as a "defeat of continuity" but, rather, as that which subverts a hegemonic, paternal (symbolic) order by allowing to the surface what had previously been repressed? From this perspective, narratives, as a particular modality of this symbolic order, are what Roland Barthes might call "readerly" texts, texts in which the signifiers themselves remain completely transparent, acting as windows through which we may gaze unimpeded at the constructs of meaning situated on the other side (Barthes 1974). Narratives and their accompanying sense of historical continuity are, in this view, illusions—mythical texts that conceal their fictional status through an unquestioned guise of naturalness. Like a film presenting as one continuous entity its thousands of frames, historical narratives similarly conceal their own ideological leanings. As texts of myth, they are acts of exclusion, "abolish[ing the] complexity of human acts" and giving them "the simplicity of essences" (Barthes 1972: 143). In this interpretation of narrative, ruptures equate to the sudden exposure of what has been, throughout the course of a story, concealed or repressed from view. Here, rupture is the destruction of illusion, the exposure of the machine.

Rose's tripartite model of flow, layering, and rupture figures usefully into Andre

Benjamin's "A Life in the Day of Benjamin André (Incomplete)." The rap is, first of all, a narrative in the most literal sense: it is the story of Benjamin's life woven together in a fashion that yields meaning and facilitates understanding. This linear sense of storytelling is reflected in the very character of his rapping as his words flow unimpeded for the track's full duration. Layering, as the component of hip hop that "reinforce[s] and embellish[es]" the ongoing narrative flow, can be considered a kind of cross-section of the music as compared to its horizontal flow—its synchronic *presence* in, as compared to its diachronic *process* through, time. Each component in Benjamin's narrative adds a nuanced layer of specificity to his particular cultural vantage point, helping to modify his story into something highly personal. As if to comment on the simultaneous richness of both hip hop and his own life, Benjamin acknowledges not only the United States ("spring break and Daytona") but elements of the African diaspora as well ("y'all from the Islands?") with reference to Jamaican dreadlocks ("similar to the turban that I covered up my dreads with, which I was rockin' at the time").

Musically, this richly intercultural life (and art) is reflected through a layering of diverse features drawn from African American, Caribbean, and the Western avant-garde. The beat is sonically quite simple, composed of a kick drum, hand claps and knee slaps, timbales, and a synthesizer groove, none of which seem to be anything other than unmodified samples. With the exception of the synthesizer groove, the layers are so timbrally simple as to evoke a makeshift rhythm section (kicking boxes, slapping tables, etc.) thrown together for the accompaniment of a spontaneous freestyler. These impromptu offerings rarely have the luxury of summoning elaborately layered and produced rhythmic tracks. On a recording, however, any amount of complexity is possible, which makes the deliberately simple choices in "A Life in the Day" seem all the more important.

The main rhythmic groove is a composite of influences from at least two African diasporic traditions: African American funk and Caribbean music. The kick drum and hand claps imply the former while the timbales evoke the latter. This composite groove, as a form of what Gilroy has called "diasporic intimacy" (quoted in Lipsitz 1994: 27), might be a gesture to Benjamin's Western upbringing ("I'm from Atlanta, baby"), his trips to the Caribbean, and/or the intercultural symbolism of hip hop itself. Together, these layers lock into a cyclic groove that remains unchanged throughout the entire rap.

But what of rupture? If Benjamin's rap flows interminably for the full duration of the track, uninterrupted in the narrative duties it performs, how then can rupture be accounted for? To answer, rupture must be considered not only as a phenomenon that can *interrupt* layers but as that which can just as easily exist as a musical layer itself, a kind of diachronic rupture interacting with the other sounds in a way that vividly captures the multifaceted qualities of Benjamin's own background and complex identity. Its presence as *difference* in "A Life in the Day" is both amplified by its alienated relationship with the rest of the layers as well as absorbed into their very texture, creating a musical space that is, in the end, richly syncretic.

From the very beginning, the synthesizer stands out from the groove of cyclical, tightly interlocking parts established by the other instruments. Compared to the rounded earthiness of the other sounds, the synthesizer's ethereal otherworldliness dominates the musical texture by its difference alone. Played using a delayed attack, each utterance of the synth slides to full volume in the space of roughly an eighth note, creating a watery blur of rhythmic ambiguity in direct competition with the precise attacks underlying the rest of the groove. The effect is only heightened by the harmonic ambiguity, which is unabashedly non-tonal. The combined nature of these traits in relation to the traits more typical of hip hop is one of unmitigated musical "Otherness." The synth, left to speak alone, is isolated from the rest of the musical team.

As a metaphor for cultural alienation, the synthesizer most readily recalls Benjamin's desire to experiment with unusual sounds—sounds possibly even derived from the Western avant-garde. It is possible, then, to read the synthesizer's unsettling effect as a strain of Otherness transgressing the boundaries of more Afro-diasporically centered forms. Yet the synthesizer's transgressions are not malicious; the instrument appears to be striving at least for reconciliation—both formally and rhythmically—with the rap's dominant groove. While its pattern is technically cyclical, occurring in two-bar periods in conjunction with the overall pulse framework, the groove's non-assertive rhythmic character and disorienting harmonic framework obfuscate the points at which its cycle returns. The result is a slight linearization of the cyclic pattern whereby the synthesizer's periodicity, in its distorting and more abstract approach, is barely perceptible or even non-existent at first listen.

Furthering the synthesizer's symbolic alienation is the musical form. At two places, the synth performs what initially sounds to be a chorus which is not reciprocated by the other parts [1:18-2:35 and 3:32-end]. The synth abandons the delayed attacks of the previous verse's accompaniment for more assertive, direct attacks, and halves its main rhythmic value from the quarter note to the eighth note, helping to create a sense of greater immediacy and increased tension throughout these pseudo-choruses. But again the chorus is not reciprocated by the other instruments. While the accompanying rhyme scheme does, at this point, employ a new antecedent-consequence pattern as well as a shift in weight to the beginning of the measure—there is silence surrounding the fourth beats—the scheme and its accompanying lyrics are uttered only once. When the synth chorus returns for a second time, the rest of the music seems to remain largely oblivious. Alienated and discordant, the synth furthers this estrangement by abandoning its assertive attacks and increased rhythmic immediacy as if unwilling or unable to identify musically with the other parts. Here, the interminable cyclic patterning of the groove and the synth's growing entropy prove irreconcilable, the synth opting instead for short bursts of discordant sounds placed irregularly throughout the measure.

From this musical perspective, the synth's gradual descent into alienation is unmistakable; even on such a fundamental level as meter, the synth shares little with the rest of the parts. Yet if we consider these same processes thematically, the synthesizer and the rest of the rap are actually kindred spirits. "A Life in the Day" is a metaphorical life in progress, a kind of narrative "becoming" that celebrates not the objects of a life's discovery but the process of discovery itself. Benjamin's story, then, is the ultimate improvisation, set out on the "ceaseless trail" which renders impossible the act of closure. The synthesizer, itself a subjective body alienated from—yet committed to—managing and adapting to its own obstacles, hardly differs from Benjamin's own introspective quest. While the qualities of the synth part may have associations with sounds and approaches of the Western avant-garde, its identity is fluid, vulnerable, and self-conscious. Through its initial attempts at joining the "cyclic" dance of repetition, the synthesizer fights against the grain of the common Western trope that arguably views repetition as a culturally regressive and fruitless activity.[2] The realization of this desire, then, as refracted through the Western teleological model, reveals an extreme hyperawareness that results from the violent juxtapositions of such disparate musical ideologies. In the end, the synthesizer recalls similar moments of self-awareness within Benjamin's story:

> ... Girls used to say,
> "Y'all talk funny. Y'all from the Islands?"
> got laughin'; they just keep smilin'. No,
> I'm from Atlanta, baby
> ...
> I was goin' through the phases tryin' to find
> Anything that seemed real in the world,
> still searching but I started likin' this girl

While this discussion of Benjamin's "A Life in a Day" has demonstrated the usefulness of Rose's model in its capacity to illuminate certain consistencies in black cultural forms, the categories it employs can be potentially obfuscating. Through such a paradigm, rupture might only be seen in negative terms, as that which "threatens" what might otherwise be pure and untouched. As we have seen, however, rupture might be just as productively viewed as that which destroys the illusion of such purities in the first place and, like the individual frames in a film, reminds us of the multitude of disparate pieces that are actually at play—and have always been at play—in social systems.

"Whether the process of mixture is presented as fatal or redemptive," Gilroy writes, "we must be prepared to give up the illusion that cultural and ethnic purity has ever existed, let alone provided a foundation for civil society" (Gilroy 2001: 250-51). The presence of the "Othered" synthesizer as rupture within the flow and layering of Benjamin's "A Life in the Day" can then be seen in positive terms—as both a realistic representation of cultural mixture within a single "space of representation" and as a reminder of the mythical nature of hermetically sealed cultures and racial homogeneity in general. Once this is established we can return to Rose's model by injecting these new, updated conceptions of identity back into the system so that they may then become the narratives to be further ruptured and refined by new cultural confrontations.

For Benjamin, the synthesizer is just such a layer of transversal and transgression. In its unfolding, its presence as *difference* is both amplified by its alienated relationship with the rest of the layers as well as absorbed into their very texture. Ingrid Monson writes: "If ... layered musical processes are conceived as analogies for overlapping social and cultural processes the possibilities of applying them to theories of cultural globalization and the problem of hybridity begin to emerge" (Monson 1999: 46). Yet in confining the presence of the social in music to the realm of passive analogy, we risk overlooking music's potential to serve as a living, breathing political text—one that can be actively mobilized as social tool. Far more than a simple analogy, music can serve as a private medium in which cultural hybridity and feelings of alienation can be safely explored and mediated. As Lipsitz suggests, "The post-colonial era is one of displacement and migration, of multi-culturalism and multi-lingualism, of split subjects and divided loyalties" (Lipsitz 1994: 29). While such fragmentation can result in an individual's alienation from his or her environment, it can also bring together unlikely pieces from disparate puzzles. Music's potential for dramatizing the collisions of these pieces should not be underestimated.

Notes

1. Through its similarity to the Beatles' "A Day in the Life," the title "A Life in the Day of Benjamin André (Incomplete)" might also invoke yet another cultural tradition: that of white, British, and American popular culture.

2. Indeed, "what recent Western or European culture repeats continuously is precisely the belief that there is *no* repetition in culture, but only a difference, defined as progress and growth" (Snead 1981: 147, emphasis in original).

References

Barthes, Roland. 1972. *Mythologies*. Translated by Richard Miller. New York: Hill and Wang.

——. 1974. *S/Z*. Translated by Annette Lavers. New York: Hill and Wang.

Binelli, Mark. 2004. "The Soul Funk Brothers." *Rolling Stone*, 18 March.

Bozza, Anthony. 2000. "OutKast." *Rolling Stone*, 23 November: 23.

Cixous, Hélène, and Catherine Clément. 1988. *The Newly Born Woman*. Translated by Betsy Wing. Minneapolis: University of Minneapolis Press.

de Certeau, Michel. 1984. *The Practice of Everyday Life*. Translated by Steven Rendall. Berkeley: University of California Press.

Dimitriadis, Greg. 1996. "Hip Hop: From Live Performance to Mediated Narrative." *Popular Music* 15(2): 179-94.

Gates, Jr., Henry Louis. 1988. *The Signifying Monkey: A Theory of Afro-American Literary Criticism*. New York: Oxford University Press.

Gilroy, Paul. 1995. "'… To Be Real': The Dissident Forms of Black Expressive Culture." In *Let's Get It On: The Politics of Black Performance*, edited by Catherine Ugwu, 12-33. Seattle: Bay Press.

——. 2001. *Against Race: Imagining Political Culture Beyond the Color Line*. Cambridge, MA: Belknap Press/Harvard University Press.

Hall, Stuart. 1994. "Cultural Identity and Diaspora." In *Colonial Discourse and Postcolonial Theory: A Reader*, edited by Patrick Williams and Laura Chrisman, 392-401. New York: Columbia University Press.

Katz, Mark. 2004. *Capturing Sound: How Technology has Changed Music*. Berkeley: University of California Press.

Lipsitz, George. 1994. *Dangerous Crossroads: Popular Music, Postmodernism, and the Poetics of Place*. New York: Verso.

Maira, Sunaina Marr. 2002. *Desis in the House: Indian American Culture in New York City*. Philadelphia: Temple University Press.

Monson, Ingrid. 1999. "Riffs, Repetition, and Theories of Globalization." *Ethnomusicology* 43(1): 31-65.

Ogunnaike, Lola. 2003. "OutKast, Rap's Odd Couple: Gangsta Meets Granola." *New York Times*, 7 September: 87.

Rose, Tricia. 1994. *Black Noise: Rap Music and Black Culture in Contemporary America*. Hanover, NH: Wesleyan UniverstiyUniversity Press.

Slobin, Mark. 1993. *Subcultural Sounds: Micromusics of the West*. Hanover, NH: Wesleyan University Press.

Snead, James A. 1981. "On Repetition in Black Culture." *Black American Literature Forum* 15(4): 146-54.

Tyrangiel, Josh. 2003. "Dysfunction Junction." *Time*, 29 September: 71.

Discography

OutKast. 2003. *Speakerboxxx/The Love Below*. Arista 50133.

A Preliminary Step in Exploring Reggaetón

Ejima Baker

The latest musical trend to explode out of the Caribbean has been *reggaetón*. This hybrid music has gripped New York and Miami and is seemingly poised to take over other popular music markets. There can of course never be a fully comprehensive definition for any music, due to the constant contact of people, languages, and the impossibility of any popular musical genre remaining static. This chapter attempts to explore reggaetón through two case studies in order to understand its musical, social, racial, and gender implications. By focusing on the music, lyrics, images, and language of two popular reggaetón artists, Ivy Queen and Tego Calderon, this study will investigate some of the central issues associated with reggaetón.

Reggaetón is a mix of rap and reggae, musics from the Black Atlantic.[1] Although the etymology of the word *reggaetón* is unclear, early references show that the music, also called underground and reggae-español, has been commonly listened to and discussed in Puerto Rico for about a decade (Santos 1996). Scholarly definitions of reggaetón thus far are somewhat cursory. For instance, in *From Bomba to Hip-Hop*, Juan Flores identifies "reggaespañol dancehall" as a bridge between black people from the United States and people from the Caribbean (2000: 138), but he does not examine the term's meanings or boundaries. In *New York Ricans From the Hip Hop Zone*, Raquel Rivera describes reggaetón or underground as "rap and reggae in Spanish" (2003: 14). Jorge Giovannetti (2003) articulates the nebulousness surrounding the term, and suggests how rap, reggae, and reggaetón are often conflated in Puerto Rico.

Popular media have offered more in-depth attempts to define reggaetón. For instance, in *Entertainment Weekly*, Michael Endelman defines reggaetón as "a Spanish-language, pan-American fusion of Stateside hip hop rhymes, Puerto Rican salsa flourishes, and Jamaican dancehall rhythms" (2004: 11). Jim Farber establishes a link specifically between Puerto Rico, Jamaica, and the United States: "Their [the reggaetón artists] raps follow the elaborate flow of American hip-hop. Their beats mimic the hard clack of Jamaican dance-hall. And their drums draw on the propulsive Afro-Rican rhythms of bomba. Welcome to the cultural polyglot that is 'reggaetón'" (2003). Jon Pareles has written several articles on reggaetón concerts in New York City, and has also defined reggaetón as a hybrid music: "The bouncing midtempo beat comes from Jamaican dancehall, the vocabulary uses the rawest Puerto Rican slang, and the attitudes and wardrobe—from athletic jerseys to Daddy Yankee's bling-bling jewelry to the rakish suits and hats of Mackie Ranks y Yaga—reflect hip-hop" (Pareles 2003a).

Academics and journalists alike describe the roots of reggaetón as rap, reggae, and sometimes salsa or other musics associated with Puerto Rico. The inclusion of salsa in the equation, however, incorrectly connects reggaetón to other popular Latin musics; salsa has very little, if any, influence on reggaetón—the characteristics most often associated with salsa, such as clave and prominent brass instruments, are missing. Rather, reggaetón is a mixture of reggae and rap, which have separate histories and social connotations.

The word *reggae* has come to envelop various types of Jamaican music; in this essay, the focus will be on post-1980 dancehall reggae and its social and racial connotations.[2] Jamaican music has changed rapidly over the past decades, from the pre-independence mento of the 1940s to the globalization of the dancehall reggae style which began in the 1960s and continues today. The dancehall gave the proletariat a platform that allowed them a creative means of reasserting a distinctive lower-class black space identity and politics. This fundamental change in the role of the dancehall occurred in urbanized places, as a result of the constant clash between the classes that occurred in the city. In urban areas, the poor were juxtaposed with the rich whom they see every day, whereas in rural areas the class composition tended to be more homogenous.

There is a marked difference in the language of reggae since its beginnings in mento; increasingly, standard English has been replaced by patois. The usage of patois articulates sympathy with Jamaican nationalism and independence. In addition, the lyrical content has become more rooted in the urban myths of postcolonial Jamaica.[3]

During the 1980s, the lyrics moved thematically from Rastafarianism to conspicuous consumption, sexuality, and gunplay. From the 1960s through the 1980s, the songs of such artists as Bob Marley, Jimmy Cliff, and Black Uhuru were extremely popular. Songs about love and/or relationships might contain sexual innuendo but usually did not contain blatant descriptions of sex or lyrics about violence. An example of the highly politically charged music of that era was "Dem Belly Full (But We Hungry)" by Bob Marley:[4]

> Cost of livin' gets so high,
> Rich and poor they start to cry
> Now the weak must get strong
> They say, "Oh, what a tribulation!"
> Them belly full, but we hungry
> A hungry mob is a angry mob.
> A rain a-fall, but the dirt it tough.[5]

The ideals articulated in lyrics changed from political enfranchisement and the paradise of Africa to the realities of present-day Jamaica. Out of this change in the beliefs of the culture, a new genre of songs called *slackness* was born. The term slackness initially meant loose morals in regards to sex and violence; however, "[slackness] can be seen to represent in part a radical, underground confrontation with the patriarchal gender ideology and the pious morality of fundamentalist Jamaican society" (Cooper 1993: 141).

Certain artists have been both denounced and idolized for their use of slackness. One of the more controversial artists is Lady Saw, whose lyrics in "If Him Lef" can be read as a feminist reclamation of the "power of pussy":

> Mate a mate a fight
> See, a gyal pussy kill her man last night
> But watch here gyal, grab up yuh buff
> I know yuh pussy fat
> And it's the bad influence
> So when me tell my mate, my man say
> Me born with the initial of success
> No guy can take that from you
> So watch Lady Saw pon the case
> Watch this
>
> If him lef
> It not my pussy fault
> The fault me pussy have is to chip the hood right
> Me possess with the good one dammit ...

Slackness was protested by the Protestant church and the Rastafarians because it openly defied traditional social, cultural, and religious mores. The Protestant Church has always had a major influence on all aspects of Jamaican music, as secular issues were often mixed with religious ones in songs (Manuel 1995). In addition, many Rastafarians, who had a major influence on the song topics during the era of roots reggae, were thoroughly disgusted. To them, the slack lyrics represented a carnivalesque overturning of all of society's repressive attitudes towards sex and the power of black woman's sexuality, and accordingly, the ideological battle between propriety and slackness was heightened.[6]

In New York City, the beginnings of hip hop were fairly similar to that of reggae (Farris Thompson 1996: 213; Fernando 1994: 15; R. Rivera 2003: 50-55). In the 1970s, the South Bronx was filled with poor blacks, Puerto Ricans, and West Indians (Farris Thompson 1996: 214), who were the victims of the dying economy and the concurrent flight of factories that left many of them jobless. As the standard of living dropped dramatically, whites left the Bronx in record numbers and the city suffered from the loss of income taxes. Within this environment of social blight, deejaying, break dancing, rapping, and graffiti blossomed into the culture that would come to be called hip hop. But despite its birth in the Bronx in a community of Nuyoricans, West Indians, and African Americans, hip hop has been mistakenly thought of by many as the cultural property of ghetto-dwelling U.S. black males (Flores 2000: 115-39).[7] As rap spread to cities where the interactions between blacks and Latinos were either uncommon or non-existent, hip hop became more and more of a "black thing," or generally associated with the people of the underclass, who often were darker than the ruling population (R. Rivera 2003).[8]

In Puerto Rico, rap was initially regarded as foreign but eventually became associated with the underground and young people living in the *caseríos* (housing projects) (Santos 1996). Since rap already had connotations of crime, drugs, and hypersexuality, it was not surprising when the music was rejected by mainstream Puerto Rican cultural purists. Rap was a music with which the Puerto Rican youth could identify because of its sympathetic portrayals of their economic, racial, and social situations. Rap tends to be very politicized, and is usually associated with the urban (black) poor. Many rap songs identify and explore racial difference; for instance Eddie Dee's "Censurarme por ser rapero" ("Censure Me for being a Rapper"):

Muchos me miran como si yo fuera un tipo sin arreglo
Como si nunca antes hubieran visto un negro
Como si fuera un delincuente
Como si con el lapiz y con mi libreta yo matara gente

People look at me as if I were some unkempt person
As if they had never seen a black man
As if I were some delinquent
As if with my pencil and my notebook, I am going to kill people.

Although rap in Puerto Rico continues to diverge from reggaetón, which is considered to be strictly party music, both styles face social pressures stemming from racial discrimination. Despite the massive social movements to instill pride in "black" people throughout the Americas (Black Power, Black Panthers, and the Young Lords), there are still many stereotypes employed against poor black people. One that affects reggaetón in particular is the theory of the culture of poverty.[9] This theory states that certain groups of people have a complex of escapism, which is both an adaptation and reaction to a marginal position in a capitalistic society. Supposedly, these people, because of their lack of "higher" culture or "proper" behavior," engage in petty crime and conspicuous consumption rather than trying to better themselves or their situation. Rather than study the social, racial, and political factors that converge to shape the lives of the poor masses of people, the conservative politicians and scholars blame disenfranchised peoples for their social situation. Consequently, the vilification of the impoverished masses has led to police surveillance of almost any sort of unsupervised activity within the caseríos such as dances or youth gatherings. This has had a direct impact on reggaetón. In 1995, the Vice Control Division of the Puerto Rican Police Department launched a failed program to take action against stores that sold reggaetón based on the claim that it was sexually explicit and encouraged drug use (Giovannetti 2003). The reggaetón artists denounced the targeted attacks on their genre of music and the accompanying police brutality, and challenged the racial implications of such actions in a community in which the majority of the caserío dwellers were black people.

While rap and reggae are reggaetón's antecedents, reggae-rap of Panama also played an important role in the formation of reggaetón. As Juan Carlos Perez-Duthie notes, "when rap next surfaced [in Puerto Rico], it showed the influence of Jamaica's dancehall reggae, heard through tapes brought by visiting Panamanian musicians (in Panama, where there's a large Jamaican [descended] population, reggae in Spanish is very strong). It morphed into reggaetón, spilling out of the ghettos and into the clubs" (2002). In 1990, a Panamanian artist named El General captivated the MTV world with his song "Tu Pum Pum." This tune introduced what was then called reggae-español. Its catchy chorus, "Tu pum pum mami mami no me va a matar" (Your pussy is not going to kill me), captivated an audience already familiar with slack lyrics. His next two hits, "Te Ves Buena" and "Muevelo," established him as a major figure in Latin popular music. In the lyrics to his song "Muevelo," he established a pan-Caribbean ownership to his music by referencing soca, salsa, and various cultural markers from both the English- and Spanish-speaking Caribbean.

THERE ARE MANY POPULAR REGGAETÓN ARTISTS, mainly male, who have established audiences throughout the Americas. Of the few female reggaetón artists, Ivy Queen is the most established and respected. Known for her lyrical dexterity, Ivy Queen has written rap lyrics for many other artists, and has been featured on a plethora of songs such as "In the Zone" by Wyclef Jean and "Jerigonza" by Dayanara Torres.

Ivy Queen was born as Martha Ivelisse Pesante in 1972 in Añasco, Puerto Rico, where she grew up with her parents. While in *el campo* (the countryside), Ivy grew up listening to her father, a singer of *trova* (a folk genre, where the focus is on the guitar, voice, and lyrics). She always wanted to be a performer (E. Rivera 2003). During her formative years, hip hop and modern dancehall reggae were born. As the sounds of politically conscious reggae infiltrated the wealthy sections of Puerto Rico and became associated with the children of the wealthy white elite (Giovannetti 2003), Ivy listened to dancehall reggae, which depicted ghetto life.

In the 1980s, reggae and rap tapes reached Ivy Queen in Añasco. By using them as a guide, she would convert the country songs she grew up with into rap songs. By this time, when rap and dancehall reggae were popular enough to make their way to Puerto Rico, they already had certain ascribed identities. Eventually, Ivy decided she had to move to San Juan, where she could further pursue her career as a rap artist (Serrat n.d.). She moved into the caseríos in San Juan, where she experienced the dire poverty that affects the majority of the people of Puerto Rico.

As in the United States, poverty is racialized in Puerto Rico, with the poorer people tending to be darker while the wealthy are lighter. Ivy lived in an environment where poverty was equated with blackness, and despite her light complexion, the poverty that she was experiencing "darkened" her. While living in the caseríos, Ivy maintained a certain style of dress and slang that was popular in her neighborhood, wearing the large baggy clothes, big hoop earrings, boots, and braids that were popular among all the fashionable black women in her neighborhood at the time. Joining the Puerto Rican rap group The Noise in 1993 gave Ivy the opportunity to travel throughout Latin America, where she became known for her performance style and lyrics.

In 1996, Ivy recorded two solo albums: *In Mi Imperio* and *Original Rude Girl*. After having been a rap artist for years, Ivy became interested in reggaetón. Its pulsing bass and the adoption of the importance of the beat or riddim from rap and reggae, as well as its usage of localized slang gave it an urban pop appeal that attracted Ivy. Furthermore, its association with the ghetto and blackness was very similar to the world of rap in which she worked. After a chance meeting at a rap concert, Wyclef Jean agreed to co-write the song "In the Zone" for the album *Original Rude Girl*.

In 1999, Ivy's burgeoning success led her to New York City where she continued to work with Wyclef Jean and recorded her third solo album, *Diva*. New York City has historically served as a center for Latin music. Its media infrastructure, recording studios, and numerous Latino enclaves have helped to sustain the thriving Latin music recording industry. It was, after all, in New York City where music such as hip hop was simply the most recent of musical fusions between Latinas/os and blacks. Latin jazz, cubop, Latin soul, and boogaloo are a few other genres born in the neighborhoods where blacks and Latinas/os lived, worked, and played together.

Although musical hybridization between blacks and Latinas/os was already quite common in the 1990s, the ideas of latinidad and blackness were still separate. While living in New York, Ivy was undoubtedly privy to the racial tensions that previous and current generations of Puerto Rican migrants had experienced.[10] It is certain that she faced discrimination, both from the people with whom she identified and white Americans.

Ivy's unique voice adds an air of blackness to her songs. Just as in R&B and soul music, there is an established "black" sound in reggaetón—often described as "grainy" and "emotional"—and Ivy possesses it. Journalists and fans alike often note that Ivy sounds like a young black reggae artist. The guttural sound of her voice combined with her intonation leads many people to assume she is a young *morena* (black girl) or, as is more frequently thought, a young *morenito* (black boy). Her voice is fairly husky, almost as if it was the voice of an adolescent male trying to sound like a more mature young man.

Yet, Ivy is indeed a woman, and as such has had to create a niche for herself. She is a female artist working in party music genres where sexualized dancing and stereotypes of females are rampant. Historically, there has been a dearth of female artists within the rap and reggae industries. Perhaps this lack is a result of restrictive social norms regarding female behavior that have been increasingly enforced in the Caribbean since the colonial experience.[11] Ivy's second CD, *Original Rude Girl,* was an homage to women such as Lady Saw, who pushed boundaries by articulating women's sexual needs and spoke of punanny [female sexual genitalia] as a site of pride and power. Ivy's lyrics in "Besame" tell a man that he is going to give her want she wants—love and a little action in the *cama* (bed), and that the encounter must be on her terms:

> *Hey baby*
> *Dame lo que quiero*
> *Tus besos, tu amor veradadero*
> *Tu eres el hombre que quiero ven a mi.*

> Give me what I want
> [Which is] your kisses and your true love
> You are the man that I want to come to me.

Having grown up in a post-feminist era, Ivy is dedicated to parity between the sexes and women taking control of all aspects of their lives. Whether discussing sex or what she wants out of life, Ivy makes it clear that she calls the shots. On her album *Diva,* she continues to explore gender issues. In the single "Tuya Soy" ("I am Yours"), Ivy informs a man that she is going to leave him if her friends see him at a club with some other chick. By establishing female independence, Ivy offers a portrayal of women that is more complex than the hypersexualized one usually offered in reggaetón songs.[12]

As a black/Latina, Ivy has to defend herself, especially when confronted with most images of women in music videos. Ivy often jokes that despite her light skin, her "pelo malo" ("bad hair," kinky hair associated with sub-Saharan Africans) assures any onlooker that she indeed is a morena (black).[13] Music videos are another arena where, as Raquel Z. Rivera puts it, the "butter pecan Ricans" are seen as "a variation on chocolate" (2003: 127). In rap and reggaetón videos, the women in the videos are there for masculine consumption, and Latinas and black women are seen as equally desirable, combining the stereotypes of a Latina and a light skinned black woman with "good hair."

Ivy Queen brings a female and feminist perspective to reggaetón, both of which are present in dancehall but noticeably absent in reggaetón. For instance, in one of her more recent songs "Queiro Bailar" ("I Want to Dance"), the chorus can be understood as a feminist anthem:

> *Yo quiero bailar*
> *Tu quieres sudar*
> *Y pegarte a mi*
> *El cuerpo rozar*
> *Yo te digo si tu me puedes provocar*
> *Eso no quiere decir que pa la cama voy.*

> I want to dance
> You want to sweat
> And stick to me
> And grind your body [against mine]
> I'm telling you, yes you can tease me
> But that does not mean that I am going to sleep with you.

As a best-selling female artist, Ivy takes her role as a feminist role model quite seriously (E. Rivera 2003).

THE MOST IMPORTANT ARTIST IN REGGAETÓN TODAY is Tego Calderon, who has received numerous accolades and become the "poster boy" of reggaetón. As a best-selling reggaetón artist, he has made reggaetón mainstream and his album *El Abayarde* was nominated for a Latin Grammy in 2003. Tego readily admits that there were many others before him in reggaetón and that he does not consider himself to be the "king of reggaetón" that the media has proclaimed him to be (Houghton 2004). Tego's popularity has allowed him unique access to the mainstream press. Since the sold-out reggaetón Summer Festival 2003 concert at Madison Square Garden in New York City, Tego has been able to work with many mainstream rappers, such as Cypress Hill ("Latin Thugs") and Big Pun ("Lean Back"). These collaborations have helped to lower the many barriers between Latina/o artists who work in English and those who work in Spanish.[14]

Tego was born in Santurce, but grew up in Loiza and Rio Grande (Houghton 2004). He attended La Escuela Libre de Musica, a high school for music in Puerto Rico, where he majored in percussion. Tego has often remarked that he uses reggaetón's mass appeal to reach audiences to which he would have never had access as a rapper (Morales 2004).

Unlike most other reggaetón artists, Tego also likes to add bomba, salsa, and other Latin musical genres to his music. For example, on *El Abayarde*, the interlude before "Loiza" is a bomba. While he maintains the characteristically heavy bass lines, usage of slang, and reggae-like vocal delivery, he may also include some brass instruments, flute, or timbales. By including these elements in his music, Tego has made his music more appealing to those who may prefer their Latin music to sound a little more "Latin" than rap or reggae may normally sound. Furthermore, it is a way for Tego to show his respect for the salsa singer Ismael Rivera, one of his main influences. By infusing Afro-Rican musical elements such as plena and bomba into reggaetón, Tego is able to bridge the musical heritage with a certain political consciousness and to use his songs to denounce the racial discrimination that exists on the island.

As mentioned earlier, race and ethnicity consistently have been central issues in discussions regarding Puerto Rican participation in the hip hop and reggaetón realms. Just like their Nuyorican counterparts in the hip hop world, Puerto Ricans who take part in the world of reggaetón "construct their identities, participate, and create through a process of negotiation with the dominant notions of blackness and latinidad" (Loa-Montes and Davila 2001: 236). Puerto Ricans often describe themselves as being a combination of African, European, and Native American. "At best, this new historical narrative ... only [serves] to marginalize Puerto Rico's multi-racial history and the painful legacies left by centuries of racial slavery. At worst, it perpetuates a racial hierarchy grounded in centuries of stigmatization and discrimination against the descendents of enslaved Africans, a considerable sector of Puerto Rican society" (Heuman 1981: 2). Puerto Rican intellectuals often emphasize whiteness, and there has been much debate regarding the amount of "black" and "Indian" blood that Puerto Ricans possess.[15]

Although Puerto Rico's identity was supposedly one that was a mixing of the African, the Indian, and the Spaniard, the emphasis has remained on the white element. Through his music, Tego refutes the elevation of European blood (and the implied and sometimes overt negation of African blood) that is prevalent in Puerto Rican society (Pedreira 1973), as in "Loiza":

Me quiere hacer pensar
Que soy parte de una trilogia racial
Donde to' el mundo es igual, sin trato especial ...
Pal carajo España ...

Orgulloso de mis raices
De tener mucha bemba y grandes narices

They want me to think
That I am part of a racial trilogy
Where everyone is equal, [and] without special treatment …
Go to hell, Spain …
[I am] proud of my roots
Of having big lips and a wide nose

As a result of his facial features, dark skin, and background as a rapper, Tego can be regarded as an "outsider" in the world of reggaetón. Indeed, the history of people who look like him has been erased[16] and those who are not ignored on a daily basis suffer the indignities of a poverty clearly tinged by racial overtones. Since he does identify as an outsider, Tego fights for those who are considered outsiders in Puerto Rico, whether they be dark-skinned or immigrants.

Due to political and economic strife, there has been a large number of undocumented immigrants, many from the Dominican Republic, entering Puerto Rico to find work. The tension between Puerto Ricans and Dominicans is a conflation of economic competition, racial bias, and xenophobia. Consequently, conflicts between the two groups arise frequently and the Dominicans are constantly being denigrated. Tego speaks to this injustice in his song "Dominicana":

Mi negrita linda tiene chiquitito los ojitos, oye
Si me tira una guiñada se va conmigo pa' Puerto Rico, mai …
Saludando mi tierra hermana, los provincianos en Santo Domingo …

My beautiful black girl has the tiniest eyes
If she gives me a wink, she'll come with me to Puerto Rico …
Hello to my sister country, the provinces of Santo Domingo …

While glorifying his Africanesque features may make Tego feel somewhat like an outsider in Puerto Rico, his background as a rapper in the world of reggaetón also augments his feeling of displacement. For many years, rappers—Tego included—looked down on reggaetón artists and believed them to be merely copying what Jamaican artists were doing (Houghton 2004). They did not feel that reggae was a music that Puerto Ricans could adopt as their own. Furthermore, the slack lyrical content also repelled a group of artists who prided themselves on their lyrical virtuosity and political commitment. Eventually, Tego would come to view reggaetón as a vehicle to spread his message to the masses.

One characteristic of Puerto Rican rap is that is it tends to be fairly political, and Tego's foundation in rap influences his lyrics. Just as Ivy Queen challenges female involvement in reggaetón, Tego Calderon also confronts popular perceptions of Puerto Rican identity. Also like Ivy, he is also somewhat older than most other artists in the world of reggaetón (both were born in 1972). As a large dark-skinned man with a huge Afro, Tego confronts people's assumptions regarding the black population in Puerto Rico (Houghton 2004). In his lyrics and music videos, Tego offers an alternative to the quintessential Puerto Rican female stereotype of J-Lo/Maria (of Leonard Bernstein's *West Side Story*). In all of his videos, people of obvious African descent dominate. Music videos are indeed a forum for identity politics, and by placing blackness at the center of how he represents Puerto Rico, Tego challenges not only the construction of reggaetón, but also the construction of a nation.

Much like early salsa, reggaetón articulates a ghetto experience that reflects the racism and xenophobia that plagues our societies. It has begun to eclipse its ghetto association to become a pan-Latin music. As a music with its roots firmly in Afro-Caribbean music, reggaetón is poised to become a pan-Caribbean music. The most obvious roadblock, language, no longer seems to be a problem, as exemplified by collaborations between Ivy Queen and Sasha ("Dat Sexy Body"), between Tego and Big Pun and Cypress Hill, and compilation albums such as *Dancehall Nice Again 2004*. These collaborations among reggaetón artists, people from the English- and French-speaking Caribbean, and rappers who normally perform in English, are breaking down the barricades that once divided the communities represented by these artists.

Increasingly, these communities are linked though mass media. One hears reggaetón on most urban radio stations and sees music videos on various cable channels such as MunDos. MunDos, which is owned by the corporate giants who run Telemundo, is geared towards Latino youth. One of its most popular programs, *The Roof*, has featured many reggaetón artists and served as a vehicle for popularizing reggaetón through the important medium of the music video. However, reggaetón has not yet received mainstream exposure; as of 2004, there is only one reggaetón video on BET and MTV.[17] Ivy Queen and Tego Calderon are able to establish bridges between seemingly disparate communities. By exploring the positive interventions by these two artists into popular music and culture, this study is a preliminary step towards further work on reggaetón's worldwide impact.

Appendix A. Examples of Politically Conscious Reggae Lyrics.

"Explain to the Almighty" by Sizzla

> Killing is not a part of our policy
> You kill a brother, explain to almighty
> Days following days,
> We heart have hatred
> Keep up your dirty ways and Jah is not respected

"Murderer" by Buju Banton

> Murderer! Blood is on your shoulders
> Kill I today you cannot kill I tommorow
> Murder! Your insides must be hollow
> How does it feel to take the life of another
> Yes, you can hide from man but not your conscience
> You eat the bread of sorrow
> Drink the wine of violence
> Allowed yourself to be conquered by the serpent
> Why did you disobey the first commandment

Appendix B. Examples of Slack Reggae Lyrics.

"Eh Em" by Lady Saw

> Dem inna style but dem style deh wack
> And from yuh see she walk yuh know da eh-em deh slack
> And all the while a wonder why nuh man nuh come back
> A ocean a swallow up di man dem
>
> Gal a lust off a mi eh-em eh-em
> Gal a carry malice through mi eh-em eh-em
> Peter waan tow offa mi eh-em eh-em
> Cause Joan and her crew nutten nah gwaan fi dem

"Can You Do The Work" by Sean Paul and Cecile

> Fi real now Cecile yuh a talk bout see what I've been goin thru
> List one bag a man like yuh deh pon mi few
> But wait till di Dutty get a hold of yuh
> Inna di bedroom yuh start call mi Shaka Zulu

"Dude (Remix)" by Beenie Man and Ms. Thing

> Gal, if yuh love holla at mi one time (Hey!)
> Holla at mi if yuh waan di wickedest wine
> I know It's been awhile but baby neva mind
> Cause tonight tonight mi a gi yuh di whole nine (Hey!)
> Yo! satisfaction a every girl dream
> Mi love fi put it on when dem wiggle and scream (Hey!)
> Well, mi get a call from sexy Maxine
> She left a message pon mi answering machine she seh Beenie

Appendix C. Examples of Portrayal of Females and Female Sexuality in Reggaetón.

"Dale Caliente" by Daddy Yankee

> *Dale caliente...*
> *Da-Dale caliente...*
> *Da-Dale caliente...*
> *Da-Dale caliente...*
> *Mama tu no tienes fiebre, pero estas que hierve*
> *Muevete esas nalgas hasta que la tierra tiemble*
> *Nadie sale ileso, siempre sueno grueso*
> *Sigo repartiendo pasto y queso*

"Culo" by Pitbull and Lil John

> *Esta tan linda, esta tan rica, tiene tremendo culo!*
> *Que rica chiquita, pero que importa si tiene tremendo culo!*
> *Hazme el favor y meneame chica tienes tremendo culo!*

> She's so pretty and nice, she has a huge ass!
> What a cute little girl, but who cares, she has a huge ass!
> Do me a favor and wriggle it girl, you have a huge ass!

Notes

1. Paul Gilroy's theory of the Black Atlantic (1993) establishes a transnational history of "black" people throughout the Americas and places the black experience at the very center of the idea of modernity. Despite the focus on the English-speaking Caribbean in Gilroy's theory of the Black Atlantic, the definition can be expanded to include the entire Atlantic. The concept of blackness as connected by the Atlantic slave trade implicitly includes the Spanish Caribbean and Latin America, even if those countries are not always thought of as

places where one finds black people. As Ruth Glasser rightly notes, "if we start with the premise that ethnic identity has no fixed symbol and is one of a range of identities that people can hold simultaneously or successively, the ethnic experience takes on a new complexity" (1995:195).

2. See Manuel 1995; Bradley 2001; Chang and Chen 1998; and Foster 1999.

3. The linguistic strategy of using patois has parallels in the use of black slang in hip hop and the chameleon-like mixture of English, Spanish, and Spanglish found in reggaetón. In a music associated with people who are constantly in flux, the manipulation of language reflects the changing of one's identity to adapt to a new situation (Morales 2002).

4. Examples of politically conscious lyrics by more recent artists appear in Appendix A.

5. Lyrics are available at www.sing365.com

6. Artists whose lyrics can be described as slack include Tanya Stephens, Beenie Man, and Elephant Man. Examples of their lyrics appear in Appendix B.

7. As a result of a long-established black/white racial dichotomy in the U.S., some Latina/o immigrants and their descendents have highly racialized experiences in the U.S. and self-identify as Afro-Latina/o (Flores 1999). The idea of Afro-Latina/o is a relatively new one, with obvious political and national implications. An Afro-Latina/o identity is part of the changing notion of blackness, which is no longer an identity relegated to only African Americans and second-generation West Indians and Africans. The usage of the identifying moniker "Latina/o" is no longer sufficiently comprehensive for those who want to emphasize certain aspects of their heritage, whether they are obvious to an outsider or not. The words Hispanic and Latina/o are supposed to encompass the entire racial heritage of the population that they represent; however, oftentimes *latinidad* (latinness) and blackness are understood as disparate identities without any overlap.

8. A comparative example is the proliferation of bhangramuffin music in England among the Indian population.

9. For more on the culture of poverty and critiques of the theory, see Goode and Makovsky 2001.

10. In New York, Ivy had numerous opportunities to observe the similarities between the social status of blacks and Puerto Ricans and the ties that bound their situations together. See Colon 1961 and Vega 1984 for discussions of racial tension between Puerto Rican immigrants and other ethnic minorities in New York.

11. For more on Caribbean feminism, see Reddock 1994, Mohammed 2002, and Aparicio 1998.

12. See Appendix C for examples of reggaetón lyrics that offer stereotypical portrayals of women.

13. See *Ivy Queen: The Original Rude Girl DVD.*

14. For more on antagonism between English- and Spanish-speaking Latinas/os, see Flores 2000 and R. Rivera 2003.

15. See Duany 2002 and Haslip-Viera 2001.

16. See Fortunato Vizcarrondo's "Y tu aguela, a'onde ejta?" (And your grandmother, where is she?), which exposes the hidden African ancestry of every Puerto Rican.

17. "Oye Mi Canto" by Nore featuring Nina Sky, Daddy Yankee, Gem Star, and Big Mato.

References

Aparicio, Frances. 1998. *Listening to Salsa: Gender, Latin Popular Music, and Puerto Rican Cultures.* Hanover, NH: Wesleyan University Press.

Bradley, Lloyd. 2001. *This is Reggae Music: The Story of Jamaica's Music.* New York: Grove Press.

Chang, Kevin O'Brian, and Wayne Chen. 1998. *Reggae Routes: The Story of Jamaican Music.* Philadelphia: Temple University Press.

Colon, Jesus. 1961. *A Puerto Rican in New York, and Other Sketches.* New York: Mainstream Publishers.

Cooper, Carolyn. 1993. *Noises in the Blood: Orality, Gender and the "Vulgar" Body of Jamaican Popular Culture.* London: MacMillan Caribbean.

Duany, Jorge. 2002. *The Puerto Rican Nation On the Move: Identities on the Island and in the United States.* Chapel Hill: University of North Carolina Press.

Endelman, Michael. 2004. "60-Second Lesson on … Reggaeton." *Entertainment Weekly,* 16 Apr: 77.

Farber, Jim. 2003. "Island Inspiration: Reggaeton Blends Musical Styles to Find its Spanish Groove." *Houston Chronicle,* 16 Aug: 9.

Farris Thompson, Robert. 1996. "Hip-Hop 101." In *Droppin' Science: Critical Essays on Rap Music and Hip Hop Culture,* edited by William Eric Perkins, 211-19. Philadelphia: Temple University Press.

Fernando, S. H. 1994. *The New Beats: Exploring the Music, Culture, and Attitudes of Hip-Hop.* New York: Anchor Books.

Flores, Juan. 1999. "Afro-Latino Cultures in the United States." Microsoft Encarta Africana. CD-ROM.

———. 2000. *From Bomba to Hip-Hop: Puerto Rican Culture and Identity.* New York: Columbia University Press.

Foster, Chuck. 1999. *Roots, Rock, Reggae: An Oral History of Reggae Music from Ska to Dancehall.* New York: Billboard Books.

Gilroy, Paul. 1993. *The Black Atlantic: Modernity and Double Consciousness.* Cambridge: Harvard University Press.

Giovannetti, Jorge L. 2003. "Popular Music and Culture in Puerto Rico: Jamaican and Rap Music as Cross-Cultural Symbols." In *Musical Migrations: Transnationalism and Cultural Hybridity in Latin/o America Vol 1,* edited by Frances Aparicio and Candida F. Jaquez, 81-98. New York: Palgrave MacMillan.

Glasser, Ruth. 1995. *My Music is My Flag: Puerto Rican Musicians and their New York Communities, 1917-1940.* Berkeley: University of California Press.

Goode, Judith, and Jeff Maskovsky. 2001. *The New Poverty Studies.* New York: New York University Press.

Haslip-Viera, Gabriel, ed. 2001. *Taíno Revival: Critical Perspectives on Puerto Rican Identity and Cultural Politics.* Princeton: Markus Wiener Publishers.

Heuman, Gad J. 1981. *Between Black and White: Race, Politics, and the Free Coloreds in Jamaica, 1792-1865.* Westport, CT: Greenwood Press.

Houghton, Edwin. 2004. "The Year Dancehall Ate the City." *Fader,* Aug: 86-101.

Lao-Montes, Agustin and Arlene Davila, eds. 2001. *Mambo Montage: The Latinization of New York.* New York: Columbia University Press.

Manuel, Peter, with Kenneth Bilby and Michael Largey. 1995. *Caribbean Currents: Caribbean Music From Rumba to Reggae.* Philadelphia: Temple University Press.

Mohammed, Patricia, ed. 2002. *Gendered Realities: Essays in Caribbean Feminist Thought.* Kingston: University of West Indies Press.

Morales, Ed. 2002. *Living in Spanglish: The Search for Latino Identity in America.* New York: St. Martins Press.

———. 2004. "El Public Enemy." *Urban Latino* 51(June): 46-53.

Pareles, Jon. 2003a. "Spicy Mix Of Salsa, Hip-Hop And Reggae." *New York Times*, 7 Aug: E1.

———. 2003b. "A Caribbean Party With a Hip-Hop Beat." *New York Times*, 12 Aug: E3.

Pedreira, Antonio S. 1973. *Insularismo.* Rio Piedras: Editorial Edil.

Perez-Duthie, Juan Carlos. 2002. "Raperos Rule: As Rap Recedes on the U.S. Mainland, Reggaetón Rises on the Enchanted Island." *Miami New Times*, 9 May.

Reddock, Rhoda. 1994. "'Douglarisation' and the Politics of Gender Relations in Contemporary Trinidad and Tobago: A Preliminary Exploration." *Contemporary Issues in Social Science: A Caribbean Perspective*, Vol. 1, edited by Ramesh Deosaran, Rhoda Reddock, and Nasser Mustapha, 98-127. St. Augustine: University of the West Indies.

Rivera, Eliezer. 2003. "Ivy Queen, diva y reina." *Impacto: The Latin News*, 29 July: 3C.

Rivera, Raquel Z. 2003. *New York Ricans From the Hip Hop Zone.* New York: Palgrave MacMillan.

Santos, Mayra. 1996. "Puerto Rican Underground." Trans. Felix Cortes. *Centro Journal of the Center for Puerto Rican Studies* 8(1-2): 219-31.

Serrat, Jaime, et al. n.d. "Ivy Queen - Reggaeton." http://www.musicofpuertorico.com/en/queen_ivy.html (accessed April 2004).

Vega, Bernardo. 1984. *Memoirs of Bernardo Vega: A Contribution to the History of the Puerto Rican Community in New York.* New York: Monthly Review Press.

Vizcarrondo, Fortunato. [1942] 1976. "Y tu aguela, a'onde ejta." In his *Dinga y Mandinga: Poemas.* San Juan: Instituto de Cultura Puertoriqqueña.

Discography/Filmography

Banton, Buju. 1995. "Murderer." On *'Til Shiloh.* Polygram Records 524119.

Beenie Man and Ms. Thing. "Dude (Remix)." Single. Virgin Records B00016MSTY.

Calderon, Tego. 2003. "Loiza" and "Dominicana." On *El Abayarde.* RCA International B0000AQS0C.

———, with Cypress Hill. 2004. "Latin Thugs." On *Till Death Do Us Part.* Sony B0001LYGW6.

———, with Fat Joe, Remy Martin. 2004. "Lean Back (DJ Remix)." Single. Originally released as Universal Records B0002L57OG.

Daddy Yankee. 2004. "Dale Caliente." On *Barrio Fino.* V.I. Music B0002IQBP8.

Eddie Dee. 2004. "Censurame por ser rapero." On *12 Dicipulos.* South Central Music B0002A2W36.

El General. 1991. "Te Ves Buena" and "Muevelo." On *Muevelo Con El General.* RCA International B000005LEJ

———. 2003. "Tu Pumpum." On *Hits.* Sony International B00009WHTU.

Ivy Queen. 1997. *En Mi Imperio.* Sony International 82412.

———. 1998. *Original Rude Girl.* Sony International 82564.

———. 2003. "Besame" and "Tuya Soy." On *Diva.* Disco Hit B0000APV8N (reissued on Universal Latino B00018U8US).

———. 2004a. "Queiro Bailar." On *Diva Platnum Edition*. Universal Latino B00018U8US.

———. 2004b. "Dat Sexy Body (Remix with Sasha)." VP Records 6413.

Ivy Queen: The Original Rude Girl DVD. 2004. DVD. Real Music/Universal Music Latino 570250.

Lady Saw. 1998. "If Him Lef" and "Eh Em." On *Raw: Best of Lady Saw*.VP Records 1516.

Marley, Bob. 2001. *Bob Marley Live*. Universal B00005KB9W.

Pitbull and Lil' Jon. 2004. "Culo." On *Miami*. TVT B0002CHI60.

Sean Paul featuring Cecile. "Can You Do The Work." On *Dutty Rock*. Atlantic B0000BWVC0.

Sizzla. 2002. "Explain To The Almighty." On *The Best of Sizzla: The Story Unfolds*. VP Records B000063DPL.

Torres, Dayanara, with Ivy Queen. 1998. "Jerigonza." On *Antifaz*. Sony International 826595.

Various Artists. 2004. *Dancehall Nice Again 2004*. Sequence B0001ENYDK.

Musical Interchange between Indian Music and Hip Hop

Carl Clements

Mainstream hip hop musicians in the U.S. have recently begun to make use of Indian music within their own productions. Although the results have often proven to be culturally insensitive and offensive to people of Indian origin or descent, hip hop music in general has had a growing influence on the music of the youth of the Indian diaspora. In certain circles, it has become a useful vehicle for encouraging solidarity against racism and social injustice, as with the music of British "Asian Underground" groups such as Fun-Da-Mental and Asian Dub Foundation. But perhaps the most effective conduit for the acceptance of hip hop within the youth communities of Indian descent is the Punjabi-derived dance genre known as *bhangra,* the hip hop-inspired forms of which have become an international phemonenon. Asian Underground and bhangra musicians of Indian descent are achieving a more balanced recognition of the cultural elements embodied in their musical products, and South Asian participation in hip hop is creating a new standard for a better informed appropriation of Indian music by the mainstream.

In this chapter I shall first address the use of Indian musical samples by mainstream rap artists in contemporary hip hop music in the United States. Second, I shall discuss the integration of musical ideas derived from hip hop into the popular music of the South Asian diaspora, particularly in England, with particular focus on the groups Fun-Da-Mental and Asian Dub Foundation. Third, I consider the impact of bhangra on the movement of South Asian hip hop toward mainstream acceptance. I conclude with the example of Panjabi MC, a bhangra-oriented British-Indian hip hop artist whose 2003 collaboration with the American rapper Jay-Z successfully entered the mainstream hip hop market in the United States.

Indian Musical Elements in Mainstream Hip Hop in the U.S.

Since the breakbeats of DJ Kool Herc in the early 1970s, the use of pre-recorded material by other artists has been an integral part of hip hop music (Keyes 2002: 53-57). With the advent of improved sampling technology and the increasing globalization of the music market, however, the question of appropriation has taken on new dimensions. Along with the inevitable problems of copyright and financial compensation for "borrowed" material, the issue of cultural appropriation has also come to the fore. Hip hop itself has become a global phenomenon, and has been integrated into the popular cultures of countries as diverse as Japan, England, and Senegal (see, for example, Mitchell 2001). Hip hop artists, both inside and outside of America, have in turn drawn liberally from the musics of many non-American cultures.

At times, such appropriation may be a gesture of respect or solidarity, as with many of the multidirectional borrowings between the various peoples of the African diaspora. As Paul Gilroy notes, "diaspora allows for a complex conception of sameness and for versions of solidarity that do not need to repress the differences with a dispersed group in order to maximize the differences between one 'essential' community and others" (Gilroy 2000: 252). In other instances, such sampling may be based on a superficial infatuation with, or even mockery of, the music of another culture. Often, the reality seems to lie somewhere between these poles.

The issue of appropriation and authenticity is complicated in the case of mutual borrowing of musical ideas between the African American and Indian diasporic communities. In the 1960s, there was a surge of growth in the role of certain aspects of Indian culture in American and British popular music, as exemplified by the Beatles' incorporation of Indian instruments and musical ideas in some of their songs, and the performance of sitar virtuoso Ravi Shankar at Woodstock. The resulting awareness and understanding of Indian culture in the West, however, was limited at best. As Gerry Farrell observes, the Indian music craze in Western pop music in 1966 "exemplifies some of the worst aspects of Western cultural consumerism, a fashionable offshoot of Western ethnocentricity" (Farrell 1997: 197). Jonathan Bellman points out the "specious connection between sitar music, the Maharishi, drugs, and the Beatles ..." (Bellman 1998: 298). Though pop culture versions of Indian religion, philosophy, and music became prominent, their reinterpretations for American consumption often bore little more than a superficial resemblance to their original sources. More often than not, India continues to be conceived in terms of "the Exotic" and "the Other."

This remains true of interpretations of Indianness in recent American rap releases. Chris Fitzpatrick, in his review of the video of "Addictive" by Truth Hurts, claims that the group conflates the ideas of the Middle East and India, and relies "on the romantic notion that the Middle East and India are inherently mystical and sexy, as if everyone studies the Kama Sutra, practices Tantric Sex, rides magic carpets, and belly dances naked in the moonlight ... For them, it simply does not matter how the lyrics translate, only what preconceptions are embedded in the sound" (Fitzpatrick 2002). These preconceptions may feed into the popular imagination, but are certainly not representative of the cultures they address.

While some idea of India is apparently useful for the producers of such songs, it seems that they have made little or no effort to understand the realities of Indian culture, or even the meaning of the words of the appropriated samples. Fitzpatrick points out that in the track "Addictive," "the sampled Hindi lyrics describe a garland of wedding flowers that are 'beautiful' but 'bittersweet,' while the English lyrics tell the clichéd 'Bonnie and Clyde' story, drug life and thug love …" (Fitzpatrick 2002). Erick Sermon shows a similar lack of understanding in his tune "React." Tina Chadha notes that "Sermon baffled those who understood the Hindi hook in 'React.' The translation goes, 'if someone wants to commit suicide, so what can you do?' To which he responds, 'Whatever she said, then I'm that'" (Chadha 2003). This obvious and even conscious dismissal of the meaning of the sampled lyrics reflects the rapper's disregard for Indian culture. The video of "React," with its depiction of camels and belly dancers and overall emphasis on the exotic, reinforces this assessment of the song.

There are some signs, however, that American hip hop artists and producers are beginning to be more culturally aware as they appropriate Indian elements. According to Chadha, "Sermon … says he didn't know his song was offensive until now [and] promises next time he'll be more aware," and Truth Hurts claims that she is working with the new U.K. bhangra producers the Krey Twinz. She asserts, "I'm definitely going to have Indian people in my video and show the culture" (Chadha 2003). And hip hop producer Timbaland, "the self-proclaimed creator of this new hip-hop hybrid" who has begun working with the Indian American vocalist Raje Shware, "says he spends five grand on Indian albums every time he steps into Tower Records" (Chadha 2003).

South Asian Political Rap in England: The Asian Underground

Of course, Timbaland's claims to have created this fusion of hip hop and Indian music ignore the longstanding contribution of the Indian diaspora to the genre. Indian British musicians in particular have long made use of the some of the fundamental concepts of hip hop, such as sampling and rapping, to recast their own music. The degree to which this music incorporates or emulates hip hop covers a wide spectrum. On one hand are tracks that seem to fall squarely into the genre of American-style hip hop, though the subject matter of the rap may address issues of particular interest to second and third generation South Asian immigrants. The group Fun-Da-Mental, which has "a hip-hop sound frequently compared to Public Enemy's" (Swedenburg 2001: 58), is a good example of this approach. On the other hand are some bhangra tracks featuring fairly traditional Indian songs with the addition of sampled bass and/or drum tracks, as with some of the tunes of Bally Sagoo or Panjabi MC (such as Bally Sagoo's "Botallan Sharab Diyan" or Panjabi MC's "Jugni").

The blending of Indian music and hip hop by musicians of South Asian descent in many ways seems a logical consequence of the interactions between the Indian and African diasporas. Despite many differences in their backgrounds, cultures, and situations, the peoples of African and Indian origin have shared similar circumstances in their colonial pasts, in their histories of resettlement for labor in the service of European and American countries, and in their common status as undesirable immigrant "Others." This background in many ways set the stage for the racially based policies and prejudices suffered by those of Indian and African descent following their immigrations into the lands of their former colonial rulers.[1]

Twentieth-century immigration policies in England and the U.S. in many ways reflected the colonial past, and were generally designed to impose a lower status on Indian immigrants. In England in particular, the wave of immigrants in the 1950s mostly comprised unskilled and semi-skilled male workers who were not encouraged to integrate with mainstream society. This situation, however, put them in close quarters with Afro-Caribbean immigrants. These immigrant groups shared a common identity as "blacks," at least in the perception of racists within the mainstream white British population. As a result, Indian and Caribbean immigrants have often joined forces to fight for their rights and their lives.[2]

Such struggles against racism have continued to the present day, and hip hop has often been employed by South Asians as a tool in these battles. Aki Nawaz, the leader of the England based band Fun-Da-Mental, is a child of working-class Pakistani immigrants (Swedenburg, 2001: 58). While Swedenburg accurately emphasizes Fun-Da-Mental's Islamic message, Aki Nawaz maintains a clear connection with his South Asian heritage. His stage name, Propa-Gandhi, and the subject matter of some of his songs, indicate a strong identification with the broader South Asian sub-continent, and India in particular. The song "Mother India" is an obvious example of his Indian affiliation.[3] While Swedenburg focuses on the Muslim women cited in the lyrics (Swedenburg 2001: 59), non-Muslim women, such as Savitri of the sacred Hindu epic the *Mahabharata*, are also mentioned. Thus Nawaz displays a non-sectarian support of strong Indian women.

Clearly, though, Fun-Da-Mental does not limit itself to a self-conception of Indianness, and their highly political message is characterized by multiple identifications. "Mother India" enlists the female poet Subi Shah for a statement of the strength and power of women and a plea for rights and respect for women. The rhythmic foundation of the tune is typical of mainstream hip hop, but the track makes use of sampled layers suggestive of South Asia. Swedenburg mentions the use of the Sufi devotional genre known as Qawwali in of this song (Swedenburg 2001: 59). Other elements clearly audible in this "extremely dense musical mix" are sampled female voice, sitar, flute, tabla, and a melodic phrase from a Hindi film. Aki Nawaz has stated that the group has "no fear of other musical forms; it can only benefit our awareness and enrich our approach to understanding other cultures" (Fun-Da-Mental 2002).

The use of Indian elements is far more prevalent in "Mother India" than in most of the group's other songs. More often, Fun-Da-Mental's sound is characterized by a mainstream, if highly political, hip hop sound. While all of the songs on *Seize the Time* use some sampled references to India and/or the Middle East, most are dominated by fairly typical hip hop textures. The group makes use of many elements that help to define its "localized specificity" (Swedenburg 2001: 58), but their association with the broad popularity of hip hop allows them to project their message beyond the South Asian community. Their identification with Islam, as emphasized by Swedenburg, is indeed a powerful element of their outreach. But their openness to diverse ideas and sounds facilitates their inclusion in movements that are important to a range of immigrant populations who are subject to racism and discrimination.

According to Ashley Dawson, this receptivity to diverse influences is characteristic of "the participants in the so-called Asian Underground," who "adopt an explicitly outer-national approach to rhythm and identity. Although they draw extensively on Asian musical traditions ranging from the classical to the popular products of Bollywood, these artists refuse to associate themselves explicitly with any particular national location or identity" (Dawson 2002: 28). Along with Fun-Da-Mental and various other groups, Dawson includes the group Asian Dub Foundation (ADF) in this category. Like Fun-Da-Mental, ADF adopts "the subaltern nationalist vocabulary of hip hop" to challenge "both the popular racist common sense of the ethnic majority in Britain as well as the forms of state repression that often legitimate such racism" (Dawson 2002: 29). Indeed, these two groups share much in their use of repetitive foundational grooves, eclectic use of sampling, frequent spoken and musical references to South Asia, and audio clips that expose anti-immigrant and racist attitudes within the mainstream culture.

Nonetheless there are substantial differences between the sounds of the two groups that help to illustrate their respective priorities. To provide a comparison, I shall examine the albums *Seize the Time* by Fun-Da-Mental and *Facts and Fictions* by ADF. As noted earlier, Fun-Da-Mental tends to derive much of its sound from a mainstream black American rap aesthetic, and as David Hesmondhalgh observes, Fun-Da-Mental exhibits "an explicit allegiance to African American Islamic radicalism, and to the black separatist politics of groups such as the Black Panthers" (Hesmondhalgh 2000: 284). An example of this allegiance is the sampling of black American voices. As Swedenburg points out, these voices are commonly prominent African American figures, particularly leaders of the Nation of Islam, such as Malcolm X, Elijah Muhammad, and Louis Farrakhan (Swedenburg 2001: 61). The title track of this album also begins with the voice of a female African American youth passionately complaining of how society demeans black children. These black American voices are invariably the voices of the protagonists. The clips of white British voices are almost always those of the racist antagonists. For example, "Dog Tribe" begins with a recorded racist diatribe, "Mr. Bubbleman" begins with an interview in which a public figure reveals great insensitivity to the deaths of foreigners, and "English Breakfast" employs a clip of a presumed former British Raj official talking of the intent to "inflict a lesson on all of India." Fun-Da-Mental extensively uses such voice clips to make its political stance immediately apparent and provide a context for the militancy of the lyrics. In fact all but three of the tracks on *Seize the Time* feature these spoken-word samples either at the beginning of the track, or as one of the first outstanding sonic events of the piece. This is a technique that has been well used by the U.S. rap group Public Enemy in such songs as "Fight the Power" and "Night of the Living Baseheads."

On ADF's *Facts and Fictions*, on the other hand, while there is some use of voice clips, no recognizably black American voices are heard. Also, these clips are generally used in a somewhat less conspicuous manner than on Fun-Da-Mental's *Seize the Time*. Interestingly, ADF's opening track "Witness," does make use of a black voice early on, but it is that of an Afro-Caribbean, not an African American. In addition, four tracks on *Facts and Fictions* feature Indian and media voices. "PKNB" features a clip of a white British voice in an antagonistic role apparently questioning what immigrants "have been up to," but this characterization is not nearly as uniform on ADF's *Facts and Fictions* as it is on Fun-Da-Mental's *Seize the Time*. Despite the fact that ADF's use of political voice clips is perhaps somewhat less prominent than with Fun-Da-Mental, it cannot be said that ADF is less political. Indeed, the anti-racist message of the two groups is actually quite similar. It is their means of delivery that most defines their dissimilarities. Fun-Da-Mental's use of voice clips expresses a clear identification with African Americans, and specifically the Nation of Islam. The voice clips used by ADF are less specific in expressing a particular political/racial/religious affiliation.

To some degree, their separate approaches suggest that the two groups are targeting slightly different audiences, or are at least seeking to appeal to them in different ways. As Swedenburg emphasizes, Fun-Da-Mental makes extensive use of references to Islam, in various forms, in its plea for resistance to racism and oppression (Swedenburg 2001: 58). Thus, while I maintain that Aki Nawaz stresses his South Asian identity, he would seem to be identifying himself most pointedly with people around the world who accept Islam as their religious foundation. There is undeniable strength in the unity that can be created by such an identification, but I would argue that it has equal potential for divisiveness. While dissent is inevitably divisive, linking religion to what is otherwise a common cause potentially limits the range of people who might be inclined to join the movement. Hesmondhalgh notes that even within Aki Nawaz's label Nation itself there were "differences over religion and nationalisms and differences over appropriate

political-aesthetic strategies particularly as regards the legacy of hip hop"
(Hesmondhalgh 2000: 297). ADF, while abrasive, confines itself to a secular politi-
cism. Any social friction created by their message would presumably be with people with whom there is already substantial tension. Rather than advocating one
religion, ADF seeks to de-emphasize religious differences in the interest of bringing factions together. This aim is evident from lyrics such as "the unity of the
Hindu and the Muslim will end your tyranny" in the track "Rebel Warrior." Given
the ongoing conflicts between these two religious groups both within India and
between India and Pakistan, such a goal of reconciliation is highly relevant to contemporary concerns.

The groove foundations and rap styles favored by each of the two groups also
seem to be connected to this idea of a target audience. Fun-Da-Mental's base
rhythms most often make use of R&B or hip hop grooves, the sound of which
seems to be an update or enhancement of funk grooves such as were played by
James Brown's and Sly Stone's groups. The tempo range is from 89 beats per
minute (BPM) to 124 BPM, with an average tempo of 105 BPM. This range is in
keeping with tempos typical of the source inspirations of these grooves, such as
the music of the U.S. political rap group Public Enemy, whose greatest hits collection *The Best of Public Enemy: The Millennium Collection* features a beat range
from 81 BPM to 123 BPM and an average tempo of 103. The predominant rhythmic textures on *Seize the Time* also tend to remain fairly conventional in hip hop
terms, with little variation in the basic groove and clear emphasis on bass and
drum sounds. While most of the foundational rhythms incorporate Indian percussion, these instruments are not usually defining elements in the groove.

In contrast, the grooves on ADF's *Facts and Fictions* range in tempo from 91
BPM to 170 BPM, with an average tempo of 131. Tracks 2, 5, 7, 9, 10, and 11 make
use of substantially accelerated or double-time grooves (the average tempo of
these six tracks is 156 BPM), which seem more aligned with the European drum-
and-bass or trance genres than with American hip hop grooves. Like Fun-Da-
Mental, though, ADF also draws freely from American funk drum rhythms. In the
case of ADF, such rhythms are often supplemented or transformed by other elements of the groove. "Witness," "Jericho," and "Return To Jericho," for example,
make use of bass lines suggestive of Jamaican dance music. The first part of the
groove in "PKNB" avoids a funk groove feeling in favor of something like an
industrial rock feeling, with little syncopation, clear drum hits on each of the four
beats, and strong accents on the backbeat (beats 2 and 4 of each measure). Many
of ADF's grooves also make use of Indian percussion as integral parts of a composite foundational rhythm, though it is arguable whether or not this component
is more substantial than in Fun-Da-Mental's tracks.

The characters of the flow of the rapping by Fun-Da-Mental and ADF also differ in significant ways. Examples 1 through 4 provide transcriptions of the first

four measures of raps by Fun-Da-Mental ("Dog Tribe," Example 1, 00:34-00:44) and ADF ("Witness," Example 2, 00:53-1:04), as well as segments of Shabba Ranks's "Mr. Loverman" (Example 3, 00:20-00:33) and "Raggamuffin" (Example 4, 00:12-00:22). While these examples provide only a small sample of the rap styles of these artists, they help to illustrate some key difference in the respective approaches of Fun-Da-Mental and ADF. Interestingly, they both begin their raps with the same figure of an eighth note, a sixteenth note, and another sixteenth note tied into the next beat (in Example 2, this figure follows the pickup notes). After this, however, there are a few clear dissimilarities in approach to rhythm. The most obvious difference is the greater rhythmic diversity in the ADF rap segment. Perhaps more significant than the diversity, however, is the beat subdivision of two thirty-second notes and a sixteenth-note in measures 4 and 5 of Example 2 (00:53-1:04). This kind of subdivision, frequently employed by ADF, is characteristic of Jamaican-derived styles like ragga. For example, this figure can be seen in the transcription segments of "Mr. Loverman" (Example 3, measures 2-4, 00:20-00:33) and "Raggamuffin" (Example 4, measures 1-4, 00:12-00:22). The Fun-Da-Mental example (Example 1, 00:34-00:44), in contrast, consists almost exclusively of eighth-note and sixteenth-note figures, more in keeping with typical U.S. rap styles.

A tonal consistency of the ADF rap as compared with a more conversational intonation in the Fun-Da-Mental rap further supports the idea that these groups are aligned with Jamaican and U.S. rap styles, respectively. ADF clearly emphasizes a single tone, with occasional shifts to one or two other tones, as is typical of ragga artists like Shabba Ranks. The spoken word feeling of Fun-Da-Mental is more comparable to the rap style of a group like Public Enemy. Here, instead of emphasis on any specific tone, there is almost constant pitch variation.

Example 1. From "Dog Tribe," Fun-Da-Mental, *Seize the Time.*

Example 2. From "Witness," ADF, *Facts and Fictions.*

Example 3. From "Mr. Loverman," Shabba Ranks, *Greatest Hits.*

I know a girl   if a   lov-in' ya look-in' for ya buck up-on the right man   a

lov-in' ya look-in' for ya buck up-on the right one if a   lov-in' ya look-in' for ya buck up-on the right man a

lov-in' ya look-in'   for ya buck up-on the right   one

Example 4. From "Raggamuffin," Shabba Ranks, *Greatest Hits.*

Lyrics unavailable

Such generalizations can be potentially dangerous, of course, due to the great diversity of and mutual influence between the flow styles in rap and Jamaican dancehall/ragga. Also, both groups display a greater variety in their rapping than this small sample indicates. As previously mentioned, the overall effect of the music of each of the two groups is clearly the result of the blending of diverse sources. Nonetheless, in terms of rhythmic rap flow and rap tonality Fun-Da-Mental is more aligned with U.S. rap and ADF is more aligned with Jamaican styles.

The above observations about selection of voice clips, tempo, groove components, rap flow, and rap tonality in the music of Fun-Da-Mental and ADF, combined with observations about the role of religion, help to piece together an impression of the manner in which the two groups target slightly different audiences. Both seem to be promoting unity against racism and oppression, but while Fun-Da-Mental emphasizes Islam as a vehicle for unity, ADF seems to cast a wider net. Fun-Da-Mental's alignment with U.S. rap seems to be closely tied to the ideology of the Nation of Islam, and the group's various musical and political interactions with U.S. hip hop suggest an appeal for a unity based on Islamic commonality. While they broaden their appeal through musical allusions to the South Asian community as a whole, the Islamic component of their message seems to dominate.

ADF, while rooted in hip hop, seems to draw significantly from more local associations. That is to say, their musical appeal for unity seems to be directed at the immigrant communities in England that are conceived of as black in the mainstream mindset. Thus, the Jamaican references in their music are likely inspired by and/or directed towards the black Caribbean immigrant community with which they share common cause. The more up-tempo drum-and-bass- and trance-derived grooves connect ADF to a broader audience of young Europeans rather than a mainstream U.S. hip hop audience. While ADF is certainly inspired by American musicians such as Chuck D and Miles Davis, Aniruddha Das of ADF comments that the group's music is based on "the kind of inspiration that isn't about emulation, but starting from your own experience, your own starting point" (Das 2001: 59). Overall, though both groups are identified with the "Asian Underground," the music of Fun-Da-Mental and ADF reveals subtle but significant differences in the orientations of the two groups.

Despite their differences, however, the foundation of Asian Underground bands like Fun-Da-Mental and ADF is a base of African American grooves, which is then overlaid with various samples, Indian and otherwise. Bhangra, on the other hand, most often employs the strongly identifiable Punjabi grooves that one associates with the genre, blending them with American or European dance rhythms. As suggested above, many bhangra songs seem to lie at the opposite end of the Indian/hip hop spectrum from the strongly rap-oriented music of groups like Fun-Da-Mental. As the genre expands, though, bhangra today seems to be providing the most fertile ground for a balanced mixure of hip hop and Indian-derived music.

Bhangra and Hip Hop

Bhangra has its roots in the folk music and dance of the Punjab in Northern India.[4] The Punjabi diaspora, particularly in England, has transformed bhangra into an internationally recognized contemporary dance music genre. Initially concentrated in the Punjabi wedding circuit, bhangra continued to feature the sounds and rhythms of the *dholak* and *dholki* drums to accompany a traditional singing style and song repertoire. Its purview began to expand with the introduction of American and Caribbean dance music elements, along with various Indian and non-Indian samples. By the end of 1987 the hybrid style known as "bhangra beat" had gained wide popularity and recognition in the South Asian youth community. A variety of sub-genres such as "rock bhangra" and "house bhangra" came about largely through the use of sampled grooves drawn from various dance styles (Baumann 1990: 84).

Bhangra-derived dance music differs in a number of ways from the Asian Underground examples discussed above. While Fun-Da-Mental and ADF often use Indian sounds to supplement Western dance grooves, this formula is generally reversed in bhangra. Despite the progressiveness of the introduction of American and Caribbean dance elements, liberal use of sampling, and increased role of production, "bhangra beat" generally retains a repertoire of traditional Punjabi songs as the core of the music (Baumann 1990: 84). Dance grooves may be added to the mix, but usually do not serve as the primary foundational element of the track. Baumann notes that "even the recordings most heavily oriented on drum machines and mixing and sampling techniques are instantly recognizable as celebrating the folk-based genre, and experts indeed often recognize them as counterfactures, parodies or fragments of less well-known traditional songs" (Baumann 1990: 88-90).

Another difference is that the lyric content and overall meaning of bhangra tracks is for the most part far less overtly political than groups of the Asian Underground. In general, this genre is more of a celebratory party music than a vehicle for political expression. According to Baumann, "the texts of virtually all of these songs are celebratory in tone, and can focus on the beauties of the harvest season, on natural and human beauty, and on a range of, usually male, sentiments about attraction, companionship, friendship and love" (Baumann 1990: 90). While the bhangra scene has grown and diversified in the fifteen years since Baumann's article, his observations remain applicable to the main body of contemporary bhangra tunes.

But while these songs may not be oriented toward social justice, bhangra is nonetheless an important vehicle for unifying the South Asian youth community. "Sociologically speaking," writes Baumann, "it conferred on the Punjabi population of Britain the numerical strength, the capital, the professional expertise, and the tendency, at least among youth, to overcome parental divisions of caste and religion by the shared appeal to a 'British Asian identity'" (Baumann 1990: 84).[5] While the music itself may not overtly encourage action against racist policies, bhangra's role in the unification of the South Asian community certainly has political ramifications. As Sanjay Sharma contends, "the politico-cultural space opened up by the pleasures of Bhangra music is a site in which an affirmative moment of Asian identity formation has been enunciated in relation to other (political) positionalities" (Sharma 1996: 41).

In recent years, bhangra has also developed a substantial following in U.S. markets. This is not surprising given that Indians are among the fastest growing populations in this country.[6] 1965 marked a loosening of immigration restrictions in the U.S., roughly corresponding with a tightening of British borders. As a result, many Indians opted to move to the U.S. instead of England. As was the case earlier in England, a large percentage of the labor class immigrants were from Punjab (Prashad 2000: 69-82). The number of immigrants continued to grow over the years, and India is now the second largest source of U.S. immigration.[7]

As the second and third generations of these immigrants began to grow up, they found themselves confronting many identity issues similar to those that their counterparts in England had encountered. For many, bhangra has served as a ready-made musical form of cultural mediation. A significant number of people of Indian descent now reside in the New York City area, and around the mid-1990s, this city became an important center for the American bhangra scene. Sunaina Maira describes this *desi* subculture as "an attempt to mediate between the expectations of immigrant parents ... and those of mainstream American peer culture by trying to integrate signs of belonging to both worlds" (Maira 2002: 42). In New York, one way that Indian American youth have adjusted to these pressures is by identifying with hip hop and African American culture.[8]

While most bhangra originates in England, Maira argues that the music and culture of the New York desi scene are "shaped by local contexts," and that "New York deejays favor remixes with rap music" (Maira 2002: 30). The British bhangra scene features a diverse mix of stylistic blending, and hip hop grooves have become an important element of the music, but rap itself has not usually been a significant part of the equation. As mentioned earlier, traditional bhangra songs have provided the dominant texts for bhangra music. The Asian Underground scene has brought some attention to South Asian rap, and there is a small scene of Indian American rappers, such as Karmacy and other groups recording on the California based record label Rukus Avenue. As Kevin Miller (2004: 15) notes, there is a growing audience for such U.S.-based hip hop artists. But they do not yet seem to have achieved the same degree of popularity among the South Asian immigrant subculture as have bhangra artists. The demand created by the growing American bhangra dance party scene would seem to be providing an expanded market for bhangra tracks that feature rap, bringing the music closer to a true mixing of South Asian and African American styles.

Panjabi MC

Rajinder Rai, who goes by the stage name of Panjabi MC, was an early pioneer of the fusion of bhangra and rap in England.[9] He states that he was "originally into MCing and stuff. But in those days ... Indians ... didn't want any Western music in their tracks ... They used to have the Indian songs and then the drums would literally just add a beat on top of what they were doing ... But like with me, I started rapping over the beats and stuff." He claims that "back in those days all the MC's I rapped with were black and I had never heard of any Asian rappers." It seems that this degree of African American influence was originally viewed as too far from the traditional culture, and he notes that "people aren't really associating me with the mainstream bhangra or anything 'cause they've always said 'P's stuff is not keeping the true roots and we wanna keep it raw, traditional'" (Panjabi MC 2003).

Nonetheless, Panjabi MC identifies himself quite closely with his Indian background. "I was very lucky," he says, "because my parents introduced me to the whole desi music scene. It was because of them that I started mixing eastern and western styles of music together" (Panjabi MC 2003). And despite his claim to be outside of the bhangra mainstream, many of his tracks seem to be essentially traditional bhangra songs with added grooves and/or bass lines. Such tracks have brought him a great deal of success both within the bhangra mainstream and, to some degree, in the broader European club scene. It seems, though, that it was largely commercial necessity that temporarily pushed his music away from his original passion for rap. Panjabi MC says that he "started off rapping but ... found that people didn't really respond to rapping so much as the actual samples ... mixed with hip-hop and stuff" (Panjabi MC 2003).

More recently, however, Panjabi MC has been able to gain some wider recognition for his rap tracks as well. The success of bhangra tracks that include rap and other elements of hip hop seems to derive both from the embrace of hip hop by the youth of the South Asian diaspora, and from the use of Indian samples in mainstream American hip hop. Panjabi MC himself attributes the popularity of his use of rap in bhangra tracks in part to the success of American hip hop artists using Indian samples in their own work. He acknowledges that "because people like Timberland [*sic*] and Dre have brought the sound in ... a lot of people are down with it" (Walton 2003). Such interest by important figures in the hip hop industry perhaps helps to validate bhangra-rap fusions to South Asian youth who identify themselves at some level with hip hop culture. It also has increased the visibility of a few Indian diasporic figures like Panjabi MC in the mainstream hip hop market.

While Panjabi MC has produced many of his own bhangra-rap tracks over the years, his broadest success has come from the American rapper Jay-Z rapping over his already successful track "Mundian To Bach Ke." The original track is essentially a traditional bhangra song sung by the well-known Punjabi vocalist Labh Janjua, and featuring a mix of standard bhangra instrumentation, the bass line from the theme song from the television show *Knight Rider*, a hip hop drum track, scratching, and other effects. The track was originally released in 1998, but in December 2002 it became established on the European Top 40 charts, climbing to number 1 in Greece and number 2 in Germany (Farber 2003). Jay-Z happened to hear it being played in a club in Switzerland, and contacted Panjabi MC to do a new collaborative version of the track. The finished product, entitled "Beware of the Boys" was released in 2003, and is little more than the original track overlaid with a fairly ordinary rap by Jay-Z. However, it succeeded quite well in mainstream American hip hop circles, presumably due in no small part to Jay-Z's prestige in the industry. Jim Farber cites this track as being the first crossover hit from bhangra, and notes that the song made it into the Top 20 on *Billboard*'s Hot R&B/Hip-Hop Airplay chart and the top 30 of *Billboard*'s Hot 100 Pop Song list (Farber 2003).

To a degree, some aspects of Jay-Z's rap echo the cultural insensitivity of the previously mentioned uses of Indian samples in hip hop. Perhaps alluding to R. Kelly's song "Snake," Jay-Z makes a few similar snake references in his own rap. Panjabi MC himself seems to buy into certain East-West stereotypes, as he claims that the track "mixes the Eastern spiritual side with the power of the bass of the West" (Farber 2003). It is bit of a reach to call this song, or bhangra in general, spiritual. Bhangra originated as a secular, not a religious, folk music, and has become a popular party music over the years. Sabita Banerji describes bhangra as "vibrant, rhythmic and joyfully hedonistic" (Banerji 1990: 208). The lyrics of the song in this track are essentially a warning to a beautiful young girl to beware of the many young men who will be attracted by her physical beauty.

These criticisms aside, there are several ways in which the rap shows at least a limited understanding of the context of the song, and perhaps the culture. The lewd and boastful tone of Jay-Z's rap is somewhat appropriate to the song's lyrics. He seems to take on the role of one of the "boys" of whom the girl in the song is admonished to beware. While this may be coincidental (such boasting is hardly new to rap), it seems likely that Panjabi MC would have explained the context to Jay-Z. The very fact that this track is a collaboration of sorts rather than a simple appropriation suggests an approach of relative equality and mutual understanding. Granted, this collaboration is a mediated meeting of cultures, as Panjabi MC himself is several steps removed from the original source material of the song. Nonetheless, the collaborative nature of the track is a step in the right direction. It was released both on Jay-Z's album *Blueprint 2.1* and Panjabi MC's album *Beware*, suggesting shared ownership of and responsibility for the track.

For Panjabi MC, this was not only his first U.S. release, but it was a track that derived a significant part of its success from the inclusion of rap. While Panjabi MC is not the featured rapper on "Beware," the track's success has provided increased exposure for his own rapping and DJing skills. A few of his other albums are now available in the U.S. as imports through such mainstream outlets as Amazon.com and Tower Records. Many of these tracks blend Indian sounds with elements of hip hop, reggae, and other Western dance styles, and Panjabi MC seems to take a more active role as a turntablist, rapper, and producer. The album *Desi*, for example, features rapping on the tracks entitled "Sassi," "Panj Pind," and "Dil Bharian" by Panjabi MC, Mister G, and Villain MC. "Intro" and "Dil Bharian" highlight Panjabi MC's turntable skills by featuring live scratching, and the blending of Indian sounds with elements of hip hop, reggae, and other Western dance styles is much more prominent than in the track "Beware of the Boys."

Conclusion

Whether or not Panjabi MC will be able to capitalize on this success to cross over from bhangra to hip hop remains to be seen. In any case, the participation of musicians of South Asian descent in more mainstream fusions of Indian-derived music and hip hop seems to be part of a changing perspective regarding the appropriation of Indian culture. It is unlikely that all hip hop artists will soon abandon stereotypical views of Indianness, but the Othered status of Indians in representations of the exotic East is becoming increasingly untenable. The growing presence of immigrants from the second most populous country in the world contributes to the familiarity of Indian culture in the West. And while their participation in hip hop may identify the Indian diaspora with the Otherness of black culture, it is at least a familiar otherness. Indian immigrants have effectively used hip hop as a means of identifying their common cause with those of African descent. As African American artists embrace the participation of the Indian diaspora in hip hop, their exotic conception of South Asians may be replaced by a realization of their shared commonality.

Notes

1. See Prashad (2000: 16) for a discussion of the shared history of oppression of India and Africa at the hands of the colonial powers.

2. For example, see Prashad (2000: 77) for his account of joint resistant of Indians and Afro-Caribbean immigrants in England against white supremacist attacks. Also see Zuberi (2001: 186) for a discussion of the black movement in England in the late 1960s and 1970s.

3. For complete lyrics, see the liner notes for *Seize the Time*.

4. See Middlebrook 2000, Qureshi 2001, and Baumann 1990 for detailed discussions of the history of bhangra and its transformation into a popular music style of the South Asian diaspora.

5. Sanjay Sharma rightly criticizes Baumann's account as being an "overly culturalist reading of Bhangra, endowing it with a unifying impetus in the creation of a unitary Asian youth identity" (Sharma 1996: 36). But while Baumann's interpretation may be somewhat overstated and essentializing, it would be wrong to discount the power of this music to bring together youth of diverse South Asian backgrounds.

6. See Prashad (2000: 69-82) for a detailed discussion of the history of Indian immigration to the U.S.

7. According to http://www.arunachalpradesh.com/immigration.html, 70,290 Indians immigrated to the U.S. in 2001, making India the largest source of U.S. immigration after Mexico.

8. See Maira (2002: 65-77) for an in-depth discussion of the complexities of Indian American identification with African American hip hop culture.

9. For a more detailed background of Panjabi MC, visit his website at http://www.panjabi-mc.com.

References

Banerji, Sabita. 1988. "Ghazals to Bhangra in Great Britain." *Popular Music* 7(2): 207-13.

Baumann, Gerd. 1990. "The Re-invention of Bhangra: Social Change and Aesthetic Shifts in a Punjabi Music in Britain." *the world of music* 32(2): 81-95.

Bellman, Jonathan. 1998. "Indian Resonances in the British Invasion, 1965-1968." In *The Exotic In Western Music*, edited by Jonathan Bellman, 292-306. Boston: Northeastern University Press.

Chadha, Tina. 2003. "Young South Asians' Love-Hate Relationship with Hip-Hop's New Indian Beats." *Village Voice*, 2-8 July. http://www.villagevoice.com/issues/0327/chadha.php (accessed 24 June 2004).

Das, Aniruddha. 2001. "Interview: Committed to Life: Aniruddha Das of the SAMAR Collective Speaks with Aniruddha Das of Asian Dub Foundation." *Samar* 14: 58-59.

Dawson, Ashley. 2002. " 'This is the Digital Underclass': Asian Dub Foundation and Hip-Hop Cosmopolitanism." *Social Semiotics* 12(1): 27-44.

Farber, Jim. 2003. "Indian Flavor Worth Currying." *New York Daily News*, 20 May. http://www.nydailynews.com/entertainment/col/story/84990p-77681c.html (accessed 22 June 2004).

Farrell, Gerry. 1997. *Indian Music and the West*. New York: Oxford University Press.

Fitzpatrick, Chris. 2002. "Boom Go the Bombs, Boom Goes the Bass." *PopMatters*, 11 June. http://popmatters.com/music/videos/t/truthhurts-addictive.shtml (accessed 22 June 2004).

Fun-Da-Mental. 2002. "Biography." http://www.fun-da-mental.co.uk (accessed 22 June 2004).

Gilroy, Paul. 2000. "'All About the Benjamins': Multicultural Blackness—Corporate, Commercial, and Oppositional." In his *Against Race: Imagining Political Culture Beyond the Color Line*, 241-78. Cambridge, MA: Belknap Press/Harvard University Press.

Hesmondhalgh, David. 2000. "International Times: Fusions, Exoticism, and Antiracism In Electronic Dance Music." In *Western Music and Its Others: Difference, Representation, and Appropriation in Music*, edited by Georgina Born and David Hesmondhalgh, 280-304. Berkeley: University of California Press.

Keyes, Cheryl L. 2002. *Rap Music and Street Consciousness*. Urbana: University of Illinois Press.

Maira, Sunaina Marr. 2002. *Desis in the House: Indian American Youth Culture in New York City*. Philadelphia: Temple University Press.

Middlebrook, Joyce. 2000. "Punjab." In *The Garland Encyclopedia of World Music. Vol. 5: South Asia: The Indian Subcontinent*, edited by Alison Arnold, 650-57. New York: Garland.

Miller, Kevin. 2004. "Bolly'hood Re-mix." *Institute for Studies in American Music Newsletter* 33(2): 6-7, 15.

Mitchell, Tony. 2001. *Global Noise: Rap and Hip-Hop Outside the USA*. Middletown, CT: Wesleyan University Press.

Panjabi MC. 2003. "Panjabi MC finds Inspiration in Bhangra." Interview at *CNN.com*. http://edition.cnn.com/2003/SHOWBIZ/Music/09/11/mroom.panjabi.mc/ (accessed 22 June 2004).

Prashad, Vijay. 2000. *The Karma of Brown Folk*. Minneapolis: University of Minnesota Press.

Qureshi, Regula. 2001. "Pakistan VII, (ii): Punjabi Music." In *The New Grove Dictionary of Music and Musicians*, 2nd ed., vol. 18, edited by Stanley Sadie, 922-25. London: Macmillan Publishers.

Sharma, Sanjay. 1996. "Noisy Asians or 'Asian Noise'?" In *Dis-orienting Rhythms: The Politics of the New Asian Dance Music*, edited by Sanjay Sharma, John Hutnyk, and Ashwani Sharma, 32-57. London: Zed Books.

Swedenburg, Ted. 2001. "Islamic Hip-Hop vs. Islamophobia: Aki Nawaz, Natacha Atlas, Akhenaton." In *Global Noise: Rap and Hip-Hop Outside the USA*, edited by Tony Mitchell, 57-85. Middletown, CT: Wesleyan University Press.

Walton, Matt. 2003. "Panjabi MC: The Underground Sounds of Desi are Chipping Away at the Mainstream." *BBCi*. http://www.bbc.co.uk/dna/collective/A926589 (accessed 22 June 2004).

Zuberi, Nabeel. 2001. *Sounds English: Transnational Popular Music*. Urbana: University of Illinois Press.

Discography

Asian Dub Foundation. 2002. "PKNB," "Jericho," "Rebel Warrior," "Return to Jericho," and "Witness." On *Facts and Fictions*. Nation Records BBNYC 028CD.

Fun-Da-Mental. 1995. "Dog Tribe," "English Breakfast," "Mother India," "Mr. Bubbleman," and "Seize the Time." On *Seize the Time*. Mammoth Records 92421-2.

Jay-Z. 2003. "Beware of the Boys." On *Blueprint 2.1*. Roc-A-Fella Records/UMG 29702 .

Kelly, R. 2003. "Snake." On *Chocolate Factory*. Jive 4812.

Panjabi MC. 2002. "Intro," "Dil Bharian," "Panj Pind," and "Sassi." On *Desi*. Import 10168.

———. 2003. "Beware of the Boys," "Jugni," and "Mundian To Bach Ke." On *Beware*. Sequence Records 8015.

Public Enemy. 1988. "Night of the Living Baseheads." On *It Takes a Nation of Millions to Hold Us Back*. Def Jam 44303.

———. 1990. "Fight the Power." On *Fear of a Black Planet*. Def Jam 45413.

———. 2001. *The Best of Public Enemy: The Millenium Collection*. Def Jam 586012.

Ranks, Shabba. 2001. "Mr. Loverman" and "Raggamuffin." On *Greatest Hits*. Legacy 061423.

Sagoo, Bally. 2003. "Botallan Sharab Diyan." On *Hanji*. Ishq 014.

Sermon, Erick. 2002. "React." On *React*. J-Records 20050.

Truth Hurts. 2002. "Addictive." On *Truthfully Speaking*. Interscope 493331.

Notes on Contributors

EJIMA BAKER is a Ph.D. student in ethnomusicology at the CUNY Graduate Center. In addition to teaching undergraduate courses such as "Popular Caribbean Music" and "Caribbean Music, Race, and Sex," she is a singer and performs a fusion of Caribbean music and hip hop. Her research focuses on manifestations of race and gender and in Caribbean popular musics.

CARL CLEMENTS is an active tenor saxophonist and bansuri player, and has performed at numerous jazz festivals across Asia and Southeast Asia. He has recorded with the jazz group Crosscurrent, and his compositions for jazz quartet can be heard on his debut CD *Forth and Back*. He is working toward a Ph.D. in ethnomusicology at the CUNY Graduate Center.

ELLIE M. HISAMA is Director of the Institute for Studies in American Music at Brooklyn College and Associate Professor of Music at Brooklyn College and the Graduate Center, City University of New York. She is the author of *Gendering Musical Modernism: The Music of Ruth Crawford, Marion Bauer, and Miriam Gideon* (Cambridge University Press, 2001) and she has published articles on Joan Armatrading, The Cure, representations of Asian women in American and British popular music, and feminist music theory. She received fellowships from the Woodrow Wilson National Fellowship Foundation and the Ethyle R. Wolfe Institute for the Humanities to work on a book on popular music since 1970 in relation to politics, gender, and race.

STEPHANIE JENSEN-MOULTON is pursuing a Ph.D. in musicology and the certificate in Women's Studies at the CUNY Graduate Center. She teaches music history, music theory, and vocal performance at Hunter College. Her research interests include women in music, disability studies, and film.

DAVID G. PIER is a graduate student studying ethnomusicology at the CUNY Graduate Center. He is currently researching the compositional strategies of experimental improvisers in the United States and Europe since 1965, and serving as the assistant editor for the journal *Ethnomusicology*. As a jazz pianist he has performed and recorded with Roswell Rudd and Jane Monheit, among others, and has produced an album of his own compositions.

A Ph.D. candidate in ethnomusicology at the CUNY Graduate Center, EVAN RAPPORT is writing a dissertation on the Bukharian Jewish community of Queens, New York, and has presented on issues of race in the work of The Residents. He has taught at Hunter College, John Jay College, and the Hebrew Union College— Jewish Institute of Religion. He is an active woodwind player and composer, was the assistant editor for the journal *Ethnomusicology* from 2001–2005, and will be the assistant editor for *American Music* starting fall 2005.

JONATHAN TOUBIN is completing an M.A. in Liberal Studies with a concentration in American Studies at the CUNY Graduate Center. He has recorded with numerous rock bands as a guitarist, bassist, and keyboardist. In fall 2005 he will enter the Graduate Center's Ph.D. Program in History.

ROBERT WOOD is a doctoral student in musicology at CUNY Graduate Center. His research interests include the aesthetics and philosophy of music, critical theory, twentieth-century modernism, and late nineteenth-century American concert life. He is a pianist and has studied with Douglas Humpherys at the Eastman School of Music.